D0947322

BOBBY

BOBBY

Breakthrough of a Special Child

RACHEL PINNEY
and MIMI SCHLACHTER
assisted by
ANTHEA COURTENAY

St. Martin's/Marek
New York

Library of Congress Catalog Card Data

Pinney, Rachel.
　Bobby.

　1. Autism—Treatment—Case studies.　I. Title.
RJ506.A9P56　1984　　　618.92′8982　　　84-18299
ISBN 0-312-08731-4

First published in Great Britain by Harvill Press Ltd.

First U.S. Edition

10 9 8 7 6 5 4 3 2 1

To M
and all prisoners of mind, body or spirit

Acknowledgements

There are so many people who have helped both during our time with Bobby and in the writing of this book, that it is not possible to thank them all here by name, but particular thanks are due to Phil, the English lift attendant who risked his job, but never his passengers' safety, by allowing Bobby to all but navigate the lift; Ann, the New York receptionist who, in the early days, made life possible for us, sometimes showing great diplomacy in the face of official hostility; the ex-policeman in New York who found Bobby and proferred advice which I followed gratefully; and also to Sue Boothby, Honor Butlin, Sheila Carter, Anthea Courtenay, Avril Fox, Margaret Goodare, Mary Ann Hushlak, Donna Hartman, Kate Kendall, Frank Marcus, Joan Robinson, Paul Tandy and John Trevelyan.

Contents

BOBBY

Introduction

It is necessary at the outset to explain the fundamentals of an 'Hour'. It consists of a period during which an adult gives a child total attention. This need not be an actual hour in length; in the Toronto Clinic we had to cut it to fifty minutes because the adult needs a break between sessions and time to clear up; the child is never asked to do this. But the child must be told at the beginning exactly how long the period will be: 'When the big hand of the clock is here, your Hour will be over.' During that time the child is free to do whatever he or she may wish, within the bounds of danger, damage or impropriety, for which the adult takes full responsibility. Once the child has grasped this concept, he gains a tremendous sense of freedom, and a simultaneous feeling of security. Blocked areas of growth begin to be released.

Certain basic principles are involved in practising an Hour. The play of the child is 'listened to'. 'Listening' is not the best word, but the English language does not offer a better one. The process is the total receiving of the child's activity with every available sense. 'Recapping' is another fundamental principle, well illustrated by Virginia Axline in *Dibs*.[1] As the child plays, his activities are described verbally by the adult: 'now you're going up the climbing frame'; 'now you're opening the door', and if the child speaks, the response of the adult is confined to repeating what the child has said, but putting it into the adult's own language. For example, should the child say, 'I made a big splash when I went into the water,' the adult can respond, 'You did make a very big splash, didn't you?'

[1] See Select Bibliography.

Parrot repetition of the child's words could sound insulting.

The adult must be strictly non-directive, never suggesting, for example, the next step in activity; never either encouraging or discouraging. This is surprisingly difficult, as is the utter concentration necessary. Such skills have to be learned, because they are not part of usual human behaviour. Another difficult principle to grasp is that the adult does not attempt to understand the child; this could be an invasion of the child's privacy.

The essence of the Hour is that the adult is *with* the child, identifying utterly with him. Children grasp this concept very quickly, and are deeply appreciative of it. During the Hour, they play freely within safe boundaries under the full attention of the adult; a genuine gift from the adult from which every child will, in my opinion, benefit. Hours are not just for problem children; they are a vital ingredient in the healthy mental development of all children. During an Hour the child has the experience of having his activity listened to without the intervention of adult views and values; an experience granted to few children, but for those lucky enough to have received it the experience causes a removal of tension, a restoration of emotional growth, and is a source of happiness.

In Bobby's case, as will be seen, I made deviations on occasion from my own usual practice. I also expanded the concept because of his particular situation. This especially applies to the many Hours which took place in the streets, subways and buses of America; a new departure in the method which created its own problems. The term 'to do a PR' sprang into being, and was much used. Hurrying along a busy street, permitting Bobby to behave in some way which horrified the bystanders, one had to develop a way of quickly explaining what one was doing. I carried leaflets which did this, and also prepared an armoury of short, quick sentences to call out as I rushed by. These public relations we abbreviated to 'PR'; they were hit-and-miss, sometimes quite successful but often a total failure. However, although this was important, the most important factor at that time was Bobby.

A useful third person in an Hour is the observer; someone to watch the perimeters of danger, damage and impropriety, and to note when the allotted period of time has elapsed. Observing is also, of course, the best way for a student to learn how to give an Hour. This extra helper is not absolutely necessary, but does provide assistance in freeing the adult giving the Hour to concentrate utterly upon the child.

1 Bobby (by Robert Senior)

It was 4 January 1977. Bobby, aged four, zoomed along the Manhattan sidewalk, weaving among the morning rush-hour pedestrians, further and further away from the 400-foot towers of the huge apartment complex he lived in. It was the coldest New York January in a hundred years, and his pyjamas were a vivid spot of yellow, bright against the grey snow.

The guards had caught Bobby's brother, Billy, but Billy was only three. Bobby had slipped through the security forces, with a strategic skill and determination remarkable in a four-year-old. Yet in most respects he was far behind normal development. Incapable of understandable speech, he lived in a world consisting of *things*, and he wasted neither attention nor eye contact on people. If his glance met yours by chance, you felt looked through, not at. People were things, too – things from which he was adept at escaping.

This determined escapee was my son. When I'd left the apartment that morning, he and Billy had come with me as far as the lift on our floor, as they had done the last few mornings. Until that day, they'd gone straight back to the apartment after I'd got onto the down lift.

This time, they had waited until I'd left, then taken the next lift down. Bobby, still in nappies and unable to communicate with unfamiliar adults, had already developed an unerring sense of geography and direction. He knew where I took the subway, and he was determined to follow me to my office, easily enlisting the malleable Billy in the project. Billy, bright but without Bobby's skill and speed, never made it through the lobby, where the security guards were always on duty. Somehow Bobby did.

Then his luck ran out. A security guard on the periphery of the complex just happened to see the small yellow streak disappearing around a corner several blocks away, and took off after it, wincing as a bus just missed it. Adult speed barely prevailed. The guard didn't nab him until he was almost at the subway stop six blocks away, having darted across two major avenues and five streets busy with heavy New York traffic.

Meanwhile, when the boys didn't return Louise had begun to worry. Thinking they must be playing in the fire stairs she had put on a dressing gown – it barely fitted her, since she was five days past the due date for the birth of her third child. She searched the two stairways on our floor: no boys. Guessing where Bobby had headed, she reluctantly took the lift to the chilly lobby to find Billy in custody, a chastened captive in his blue pyjamas, looking as cherubic as only he could when there was trouble in the air. At the same moment the guard entered the lobby with Bobby slung over his shoulder, raging and howling.

Louise, shivering in her dressing gown, gave the guards her usual embarrassed thanks, before taking one boy firmly by each hand, not to let go of them again until they were safely locked in our apartment.

The guards were well trained and, for the most part, kind-hearted but Bobby was a *very* strange little boy, and similar scenes had been occurring with increasing frequency of late. Louise felt more embarrassment each time. Though most of them never said anything directly, they were giving her looks and sometimes dropping hints that she was a neglectful mother who was making their life more difficult. They were, after all, employed to protect the tenants from muggers and burglars, not from two very small boys.

She gave me the colourful details after dinner that night; we never had a chance to talk before the boys were in bed.

That was ruled out by the non-stop conversation which they conducted at high volume before and during dinner in a jabber language known only to the two of them.

Soon after dinner, Louise cut the threads that sewed our sons into their one-piece jumpsuits, washed them, changed their nappies, then resewed them into their pyjamas for the night. After singing them their 'night-night' song in the room they shared, she turned on the tiny television set on its high shelf; this gave them something to focus on and to distract them from fighting each other until they dropped off, when we turned it off from another room. Then she turned out the light and set the heavy latch which kept the door about four inches open, too small an opening for the lively lads to wriggle through. At last we could relax and discuss the day's events in detail.

Louise and I had been married just five years, and our third child would be born any day. Thanks to an amniocentesis test, we knew it would be a girl – something to look forward to after the exhilaration of living with what the neighbours had named 'the Sunshine Twins'. But for a long time now we'd been wondering how we were going to cope; as the boys daily grew stronger, more mobile and more sophisticated, the problems were more severe. Louise, heavily pregnant, had been pulled over more than once when trying to hold on to them. How was she going to take care of an infant as well as these two? Once again, we tried to find a solution. Once again we wondered what we had done to produce two totally unmanageable, self-directed children.

Bobby was born on 22 October 1972, ten months after our wedding. I'd just turned forty and Louise thirty when we married; I was practising law and we had met through our interest in music. I already had a son, George, five and a half years older than Bobby, who continued to live with his mother but came to stay with us just about every other weekend.

As a baby Bobby showed no sign that he was going to

create havoc in our lives. His birth had not been completely normal: just before delivery, the doctors had found meconium in the amniotic fluid, a sign of stress. The baby's umbilical cord was tangled around his neck, threatening to cut off his oxygen supply, while the external cardiac monitor showed a rapid and increasing heartbeat. The obstetrician used lower forceps to hasten the birth. But all the post-natal checks were positive, and mother and baby left the hospital for home four days later.

Bobby was an attractive baby, peaceful and calm-looking, and he grew rapidly into an apparently normal, happy infant. Louise found him very easy to look after; he was alert, good-humoured, chortling at the toys in his playpen and crying only when hungry or cutting a difficult tooth. She cuddled him while giving him his bottle, and when he was old enough to be fed sitting up she would talk to him as she put the spoon into his mouth – he always happily ate everything she gave him. She did notice at these times that his dark brown eyes seemed to look through her rather than at her, and she invented a game in which she put her face close to his, saying 'Eyes', as she tried to meet his gaze. He would keep looking in her direction, but she still had the sense that he was looking past her. She was puzzled by this but not upset; she decided he was more interested in thinking his own thoughts than in playing a game with her.

He was always observant of the *things* around him; in the spring he would watch with fascination the play of light on leaves, and would have fun biting the lion on his quilt, with enthusiastic cries of 'Aargh!' At the beginning of June 1973 he started to sit up in his playpen; on 9 June he stood up and on 16 June we saw him take his first steps, holding onto the playpen rail. (He bypassed the crawling stage completely; before learning to walk he slithered around the floor on his bottom.)

By 11 October 1973, when Billy was born (a very easy birth), Bobby, now eleven and a half months old, seemed on the path of normal infant development. There were two exceptions. Although he babbled to himself, he hadn't yet learned to use words, except for 'Mama', which he only used as a cry of protest, and 'Bob-Bob-Bob', which he repeated while looking at himself in the mirror. Secondly, we were beginning to notice that he wasn't relating to us, or anyone else, as people.

As I had with George, now six, I kept detailed notes on Bobby's progress – weight, height, diet, development stages, 'episodes', etc. I couldn't help comparing Bobby's slowness to speak with George's precociousness in this area. But I kept telling myself what all the child-raising authorities emphasize: each child goes at his own rate; there are no 'official' timetables of ages by which all normal children *must* crawl, stand and speak. We ended up fairly relaxed about speech.

For the same reasons, we weren't too concerned at first at Bobby's increasing tendency to focus on *things* and ignore people. We thought it 'cute' when he'd take an adult's hand and place it on a doorknob he wanted opened, or a toy he wanted operated. At the time, it didn't strike us that he regarded adults just as he regarded *things*: environmental objects to be manipulated for his benefit.

Looking back now, I can see that I 'interpreted' Bobby's development in ways which were prematurely optimistic. Any parent would have trouble recording the development of his own child with clinical accuracy, because of the heavy emotional involvement. I had a tendency to resolve ambiguities in favour of 'normal' development.

As Bobby started his second year, we began to notice an emerging pattern of repetitive or perseverative conduct which he engaged in more and more frequently. I timed him once as he stood at the entrance to the bedroom he shared with Billy, opening and closing the door for almost thirty minutes – open, close, open, close. A less obvious example of the same pattern was his habit of putting things in disarray –

objects on a table, books on a shelf, his toys on the floor – and then carefully putting them back exactly the way they had been, before repeating the whole sequence again and again.

But he did all this with a smile, chuckling – how could anything have been seriously wrong with such a good-natured little boy? We enjoyed his agility and obvious intelligence as he opened and closed everything, operated all devices within his reach, climbed everything climbable.

We had some bookcases reaching up fifteen feet to the ceiling: Bobby would somehow climb all the way to the top and hang there by his fingers and toes like a little monkey, while Louise stood below wondering how he did it and afraid he would fall: he never did. He also climbed up the window, getting finger and toe holds on the narrow wooden strips, like a miniature Spider Man.

Louise tried not to restrict his activities. In the mornings he would be running up and down the living room till 11.30 – he never walked at any time, he always ran. While she took care of baby Billy and fixed lunch she would put him in his room to play – and to climb the windows. In the afternoons she would play with him and his toys on the floor. She noticed, still without worrying, that he would arrange his toys into patterns rather than using them as they were designed to be used, and felt in these games that she was being treated much as one of the toys. She began to feel a separateness about him: most babies start out by feeling that they are part of their mothers and, as they discover they can do things by themselves, learn that they are separate people. Without fully formulating the idea at the time, Louise had a sense that Bobby had been separate from the start.

It was after Billy started to sit up, at about eight months, that Louise began to notice how differently the two brothers responded. With each seated in a high chair, she could spoon-feed them at the same time – a spoonful in each mouth in turn, any departure from this alternation producing howls from the neglected one. She could now see that there was a noticeable difference in eye contact and responsiveness. Bobby sat there being fed, taking no notice of Louise or Billy, whereas Billy looked at her, babbling, involved in everything that was going on. Louise had been trying to teach Bobby to feed himself, guiding the spoon in his hand, but he had no interest in learning. Billy quickly overtook him, learning to feed himself while his older brother was still being spoon-fed.

Bobby ate heartily enough, with no pickiness about food – although when he was nearly two we began to be concerned about his habit of eating fuzz from his acrylic blanket, which ended up looking like swiss cheese. He also chewed his clothes. The doctor, however, assured us that a diet of fuzz wasn't going to harm him.

Of much more concern to Louise were the tantrums that he began to throw at this time. For apparently no reason at all Bobby would suddenly let out a piercing shriek, clench his fists, screw up his face, and throw himself down on the floor where he screeched, kicked and raged for ten to fifteen minutes. I never saw this happen, and when Louise told me about it I felt that he was just taking some kind of alternative course to the same destination. Louise, however, who had to witness the tantrums, began to think that there was something wrong with her child, perhaps seriously wrong.

By the time Bobby was two, one-year-old Billy was catching up fast in size, and people began to take them for twins. Since they were almost the same size, Louise began buying them matching clothes, for convenience and inter-changeability. Bobby had already developed the enjoyable pastime of undressing both himself and Billy, so to forestall this she chose one-piece jumpsuits, which she pinned closed at the neck.

By now, Bobby was talking continuously, but only to Billy, in a language of his own creation. It had all the cadences of English, and even a few English words dropped in, and he soon had Billy speaking it too. To us it was totally unintelligible. As Louise wheeled them along the street on outings in their double pushchair they kept up their babble in this private language, simultaneously reaching out to grab everything within reach, including each other's hair. If Bobby needed to communicate his needs to either of us, he'd do it by pantomime or partial acting-out – putting the parental hand on a doorknob.

In November 1974, a month after his second birthday, Bobby made the first of his serious 'escape' attempts, which were later to evolve into schemes of baroque elaboration. At the time, we lived on the first two floors of a brick terraced house in a quiet residential section of Brooklyn. There was a garden at the back where the boys could play, but what Bobby wanted was the street.

One day I watched as he quietly built a platform against the apartment door so he could reach the door lock. Thinking no one was watching, he climbed up silently, carefully unlocked the door, climbed down, opened the door and went out into the hall, where he unlocked the outside door (this was one he could reach) and zipped down the stairs to ground level. Here he was stymied by a gate which he couldn't figure out immediately. At that point I brought him back, protesting, into the house.

After that first attempt, worried about what might happen if he tried it when we were asleep, we put a large eight-inch hook on the bedroom door which permitted the door to be kept rigidly open at about four inches, and enabled us to hear any noises. This seemed the only way to forestall unauthorized midnight departures.

A month or so after this, both boys fell sick with a fever and stomach upset lasting about four days. Bobby was the first to succumb, and concerned about his becoming dehydrated we continued to feed him his regular milk bottle. He couldn't keep it down, and on the third day we started giving him apple juice instead. When Billy caught the same illness we switched his milk bottle to water immediately, but with Bobby the damage had been done; probably associating milk with throwing up, he would never touch it again.

I don't know if there was a connection, but it was after this that Bobby began to be increasingly picky over his food, eventually reaching the point where his diet was voluntarily restricted to apple juice (no water), spaghetti, frankfurters, hamburgers, cookies, no vegetables except for French fried potatoes and no fruit except for bananas. There was no way he could be cajoled into eating anything he didn't want to, any more than into doing anything else he didn't want to.

Thanks to the prevailing good humour of the two boys, the predominant mood usually seemed one of manic cheerfulness. Listening one day to the Mahler Third Symphony, the boys spontaneously began to rock in unison to the rhythm of the march movement. A short while later they began to rock back and forth again, during the *giga* of Bach's Sixth Brandenburg Concerto. This time Louise and I couldn't help joining in, and the four of us sat rocking to the Bach.

Between Bobby's second and third birthdays, Louise and I began to voice the question we'd avoided: was there something 'wrong' with Bobby? Our paediatrician, modern but relaxed, didn't *quite* think so. 'He's hyperactive, but otherwise in good shape. Don't worry; just give him plenty of attention. He's choosing not to talk because he doesn't need to. He understands perfectly everything that's said to him. His hearing and other faculties all test out normal.' Maybe so. Not wanting to invent problems, Louise and I decided to give him a little more time.

In August 1975 we moved from our apartment in Brooklyn to a mid-Manhattan high-rise apartment complex; like all such buildings in New York, it had its own security force, and restricted access to the lobbies. It was a new development, and we were the first to occupy our sunny, large apartment. When we moved in it was clean and beautiful, by contrast with the old house in Brooklyn, and we hoped we could keep it that way.

With Bobby approaching three, his quirks, no longer

camouflaged by infancy, became more apparent – and some of these were definitely unappealing. Moving into the large complex in a high-density area also brought Bobby up against greater restriction, on which his increasingly anti-social behaviour was to make more and more of an impact.

On the more positive side, although he still wasn't talking, he knew all his letters and numbers. He had always had alphabet books and blocks with letters and numerals, and Louise had tried pointing these out to him. He never gave any indication that he had heard her. So when he began pointing to the apartment number in the lift, mumbling ''elve', and indicating that he knew all his numbers, it was as if he had somehow taught himself. Louise's teaching had probably been reinforced by television, with its educational programmes and particularly the game shows, which were full of numbers and which Bobby watched avidly.

He was not yet toilet-trained. Louise had started trying to toilet-train him when he was two and a half. She had read that if, at this age, the child hasn't shown a desire to use the toilet, the parents should give him a gentle push in that direction. Bobby understood exactly what he was meant to do in the bathroom, but simply refused to do it, and continued to wet and soil himself after he came out. Louise found it very tiresome to keep on trying with somebody who knew perfectly well how to do the whole operation but wasn't interested, so she abandoned these attempts, waiting for Bobby to decide, 'I think I'll start using the toilet today.' He seemed to learn things in this way, when he was ready. But he continued not to be ready, and when Louise tried to toilet-train Billy she was equally stymied. She could talk to Billy and get a response, but by this time he was completely under the influence of his brother, even intimidated by him. He, too, sat on the toilet seat not doing anything.

Nevertheless, they both developed a fascination with faecal matter. Bobby had long since mastered safety pins, and whenever he was with Billy, he'd quickly get his own and Billy's clothes off. One of his favourite pastimes was to reach into his (or Billy's) nappies for some faecal matter he could roll into little balls to be flung at the walls and ceiling. Very difficult to scrape the stuff off a textured ceiling. The resourceful Louise took to sewing them into their one-piece jumpsuits. This kept Bobby from stripping himself and Billy, but somehow the resourceful Bobby would manage to get his small hands into his or Billy's nappies for a fresh supply of ammunition. I would regularly come home from the office to find Louise exhausted and in tears having had to wash the stuff off not only the walls and ceiling but the floor, mesh window screens, Lego toys, cots, and the boys themselves who had shampooed their hair with it.

With the need to change nappies, Louise was sewing each of them into his clothes six times a day – and it wasn't only clothes they had to be sewn into. While in the pushchair, Bobby had taken to hitting and biting Billy, and pulling his hair as he sat across from him. Louise found the only way to prevent this was to sew them both to harnesses attached to the pushchair. She got a lot of sewing practice.

When Louise did take them out to the stores she was limited by the size of the double pushchair which was too heavy to negotiate through some doors or up and down steps. Leaving them outside was not something she wanted to do, but once when she had to, in order to go into a lamp store, Bobby disengaged the brake of the pushchair and Louise had to run after them as they careered joyfully down the hill. Taking them out on foot was another perilous adventure: they were into everything, pulling merchandise out of drawers, totally unresponsive to Louise's attempts to control them. (There were some stores from which they were barred.) Bobby's obsession with patterns and rules, increasingly apparent, showed on these outings too; he would not permit the accompanying adult to take him the 'wrong' way down a one-way street, but would insist by pantomime on being taken in the 'right' direction.

In the new apartment Bobby and Billy shared a bedroom, as they had before. It had a large window, consisting of a single pane of glass about three feet by four feet, pivoting open vertically. We kid-proofed it so that it opened only three inches, enough for air but not a small child. Before they'd been in the room twenty-four hours, all toys and books small enough to fit through a three-inch opening had been jettisoned out of the window – a considerable volume of articles, some of them heavy. Luckily for us, none of this material had hit anyone on the street far below, or at least it hadn't hit anyone who survived to trace it back to our apartment.

This was the least of the window problem. The sill was wide enough for the two boys to get up on. In our first few days in the new apartment we had several visits from the security men, in response to telephone calls from alarmed neighbours who could see Bobby and Billy fighting on the sill. The tempered glass was *probably* strong enough to withstand their combined seventy-five pounds, but perhaps not the metal toys with which they whacked away at each other. It was quite easy to imagine two small bodies flying through showers of broken glass to smash on the concrete below. I soon covered the window with a metal mesh screen to prevent disaster, and installed the door hook from their old bedroom, so the door could be opened just short of head width.

It was around this time that Bobby's expression changed. During his first two years his joyous smile and general air of bonhomie had added a charm to his activities. Now he smiled less; his expression became pensive and withdrawn, with lips pursed tight, his eyes now clearly refusing to meet yours. His aggression towards Billy was escalating too: sometimes, hearing a shriek from their bedroom, we would go in to find deep teeth marks on Billy's arms or face. Billy was beginning to be frightened of Bobby, and at the same time almost a slave to him, copying his speech, his gestures, his activities, and his constant motion. Bobby was *never* at rest, perpetually running back and forth, and impossible for Louise to restrain when she took him out.

In the months past Bobby's third and Billy's second birthday, we began to be seriously concerned about Bobby's 'hyperactivity' and his failure to speak and socialize himself. By now he was speaking, after a fashion; but only when he felt like it, or when it was absolutely necessary, and only his parents could understand him. He'd say things like 'Coat car bye-bye office' ('Put my coat on me, get a taxi, and let's go to your office'), 'Mama bye-bye shower' ('Mama is taking a shower'), and 'Bye-bye keen (clean)' ('Let's go do the laundry in the laundry room on the third floor').

The only time he spoke clearly was when he played at re-enacting a TV quiz show. The two boys would start the game between themselves and then draw in Louise and me, giving us instructions to 'be happy' because we'd just won a million dollars, or 'be sad' because we had lost. We would assume the appropriate expressions. This did not mean that Bobby was communicating with us as people: we were playthings, extensions of the TV set.

We could no longer blind ourselves to the fact that there was something wrong with Bobby, and our paediatrician was no longer quite so sanguine that Bobby would eventually 'straighten out' without specialized help. His first thought had been that Bobby was simply hyperactive: now he began to wonder if there was a hearing problem, so we started by taking him to a Speech and Hearing Clinic at the good teaching hospital where he'd been born. (In the waiting room Bobby, in a harness and on a leash, almost pulled Louise out of her chair.) His physical faculties tested out without anomaly or abnormality. The tester remarked that he was 'bright' for learning the test games so rapidly. Our doctor's next suggestion was that we take him to see a well-known paediatric neurologist, which produced the all-but-certain diagnosis: autism.

A terrifying word for a parent to hear. Louise and I were reasonably well-read, and all the experiences of the last three years seemed to support the diagnosis: the avoidance of eye contact, the concentration on *things* instead of people, the perseverative conduct, the total absorption in simple mechanical processes. We'd read that autism was incurable. It also required life-long institutionalization, especially tragic because autistic children, were usually far above normal in intelligence.

Off we went in search of a second opinion, a third opinion, whatever it took to get a more acceptable verdict. A celebrated child psychiatrist, Viennese to her core except for the absence of a beard, said he just *might* be autistic, but in any event needed a heavily structured environment, which he might get in a specialized school. Another child psychologist was in agreement with the first. Yet another said essentially the same thing, stressing the need for a heavy behaviour modification environment. Ditto several others.

We soon got to see what a 'heavy behaviour modification environment' was. At the neurologist's suggestion, we took Bobby to see the director of the children's programme at a huge and authoritative teaching institution.

This doctor had no uncertainty – Bobby *was* autistic. He'd never be 'normal', but his best chance for getting to the point where he *might* be able to function on his own as an adult was to be enrolled in her programme, preferably on an institutionalized basis. We looked around the hospital floor which housed her 'programme', and watched children of assorted ages go through activities where every second of their time was relentlessly pre-programmed. Some were 'playing', as the keepers physically forced them through various activities. Some were eating, the hands of the attendants on their wrists, guiding the utensils from plate to mouth and back. Overall, the atmosphere was that of a maximum-security prison, with bars, locks, and peep-holes fit for death row. The authorities there were enthusiastic about the benefits of behaviour modification, and we could almost hear the crack of the whips. We wouldn't let Bobby spend five minutes in that place.

As if this wasn't enough, Louise was pregnant again. Just thirty-five, she took the amniocentesis test recommended for 'elderly' mothers; the baby girl would have no birth defects, and would be born on 30 December 1976.

By this time I had a job which involved much travelling to California and Europe. On most of these trips Louise was left alone with Bobby and Billy. How could Louise handle a third child on top of the two she had? She couldn't even take them out of the apartment unless they were sewn into the pushchair. On foot, they would have immediately taken off in opposite directions.

The apartment complex had two miniature but well-designed playgrounds, each with a children's wading pool. Whenever Louise took the boys there, they had no concept of playing or talking with the other children. Instead, Bobby would march up to any child who had a toy he fancied and seize it, to the point of knocking children off riding toys so that he could ride them, countering any opposition by screaming, biting and hitting. The other mothers, outraged that Louise would 'let him get away with *anything*', ganged up on her. One day as she was sitting in the playground, a group of mothers came over and stood in a semicircle in front of her. They told her in no uncertain terms that they did not want 'that child' in the playground any more; it wasn't fair to the other children. Whatever problems she had, they should not be expected to deal with them or risk the safety of their own children. Any more such incidents and they would report her to the management of the apartment complex. Louise collected the children, luckily without an incident, and removed them with dignity, restraining her tears until she was back in the apartment.

At the same time, the sales-people in some of the stores she shopped in forbade her on their premises if 'that child' was with her. Louise, not the most assertive and self-confident person in the first place, found these experiences crushing and indescribably embarrassing, evidence of her inadequacy as a mother.

I too found these encounters embarrassing when they happened to me. On my days at home, I made it a point to go out for a ramble with both of the boys, but never with both at once. I'd take one to the store with me, the other to the laundry room, then boy one on my next trip outside the apartment. One boy at a time was manageable, and I tried to talk with them, though Bobby was not what you could call a conversationalist. Still, I sometimes got glimpses on these walks of the intelligence that he preferred to keep hidden from the world. Bobby had always been interested in words, though as sound phenomena rather than as tools of communication. One time, going down with him in the lifts, he pressed the button for the lobby saying 'Down, down!' This triggered in my mind a passage from *Richard II* which I paraphrased out loud, hoping to open a conversational channel: 'Down, down, into the baser court, like the cart of glistering Phaeton.' Bobby didn't react until we reached the lobby floor, when he repeated the quotation perfectly. He said it again several times in the following weeks, always when we were going down in the lift. He also asked me – and such requests for information were very unusual – 'What means baser court? What means a Phaeton?' Something about the rhythm of the words had caught his imagination.

There were few such opportunities for me to experience fatherly pride. In the autumn of 1976, Bobby, a four-year-old in nappies who couldn't talk intelligibly, was becoming more and more unmanageable. He bit and struck Billy constantly. Once, while I was in Europe for three weeks, he broke up both the cots, practically into their component pieces of wood. These were made in Finland of heavy birch, tongue-and-grooved, screwed and glued, and I wouldn't have thought an adult male could have broken them up without tools. Louise attempted, pregnant as she was, to repair them with wire, but Bobby re-demolished them each time. The boys slept on their mattresses on the floor until I returned to re-glue and re-screw the cots, after which we fixed them to the baseboards with eye rings and heavy wire.

As Louise slowed down because of her pregnancy, Bobby speeded up, and began to 'escape' more often from the apartment, although he usually stayed on our floor playing in the fire stairs.

Sometimes they went further afield, to the basement or the laundry room, often getting caught by the security guards. The laundry room was on the third floor, which gave onto a large open terrace with sizeable trees planted around it. In the centre was a glass roof over the lobby. More than once, Bobby and Billy found some fairly large stones in the landscaped portion and started throwing them either onto the glass roof, or three flights down onto the sidewalk where people were walking by. Several times the guards in the lobby looked up to see their shadows: once Bobby started walking out onto the glass and an alarmed guard rushed upstairs to retrieve him.

It was a common experience for Louise to open the front door to a security guard returning a screaming child and recounting some terrible story about how disaster had been narrowly averted and she shouldn't let them do it again. Most of the guards were polite, but one of them had no hesitation in letting her know that because of her negligence the guards had to do the job she should be doing. They had a legitimate point, but their attitude did not make Louise feel any better.

In October 1976 some of the pressure was temporarily relieved when we hired Doreen, a woman from the Jamaican hill country, as a part-time housekeeper. She came at noon on weekdays and stayed until 7 p.m., about the time I got home. When she first came Louise tried to explain the problem of the two boys. Communication was difficult because of Doreen's strong accent but after a while she found her own way of handling the children. She gave them baths together every night, a relatively peaceful activity, as they enjoyed playing with the water and toys. She was a big, strong woman, and was quite warm with them although they gave her a lot of trouble and tried her patience. However they allowed her to do things with them that they would not allow Louise to do. When neither Doreen nor I was there Louise was finding her daily routine almost more than she could handle. She kept going because she had to.

On 8 January 1977, only four days after that freezing trip to the lobby to retrieve the recaptured Bobby, Louise went into hospital to give birth to our daughter Abigail. During her time in the hospital, four days of treasured rest, Louise's parents moved into our flat to help me and Doreen with Bobby and Billy.

Both boys were pleasantly excited when Louise and the new baby came home on the 12th. They wanted to hug and kiss their new sister, and were disappointed when we wouldn't put her down on the floor so they could play with her. Bobby seemed equable and accepting, but that night had an unusually strong tantrum.

Three days later, on Saturday (no Doreen) the 15th, I woke up with a recurring slipped disc condition. For the first time in my life, it was so bad I couldn't walk, couldn't bear any weight at all on my feet. I could move away from the bed – in excruciating pain – only by resting my upper torso on the seat of a straight chair, and sliding the chair along the wood floors.

On 1 March Bobby made the longest speech he'd ever made to me, completely out of the blue:

'Go to Brooklyn. Go to the house in Brooklyn. Go down the stairs. Go out the window. Go out.' (Mimes lifting the window and stepping out.) 'Go out. Okay. Close it. Lock it.' (Mimes closing and locking window.) 'Go downstairs. Okay. Open gate. Big windows. Right. Big windows. Go to

Brooklyn. Baby Bobby. Go to Brooklyn with' (pointing) 'piano, radio, that, that, that.' (Pointing at those but only those objects which had been in our Brooklyn apartment when we left over a year and a half before.)

Except for Louise and me, no one could have understood him, but he left no doubt that 'Baby Bobby' would like to return to the good old days in Brooklyn.

As winter hung on, the pressure on both Louise and me was enormous, unremitting and claustrophobic, despite Doreen. We were in some desert fort, our water gone, thousands of frenzied Arabs firing at us, and no relief column in sight.

All the pressure seemed to originate with Bobby. His care took a disproportionate amount of our time, attention and money. What about the other children? What was Bobby doing, as a model, to Billy, and what would he do to baby Abigail? He was a unique, extraordinary child, but totally in his own universe. He wasn't amenable to conventional restraints, even the minimal ones necessary for his own safety and that of others.

As a practical matter, the problem was no longer just Bobby. He and Billy were now a team act. The hyperactive Sunshine Twins, four and three, were still unhousebroken, sewn into their clothes, covering the walls with writing and the ceilings with poo-poo, shrieking happy or shrieking mad, ready to dart like mice through any open – or openable – door. We loved Bobby, but it seemed that Billy, essentially a normal child, was being sacrificed to him, and that Abigail could follow the same route.

We were beginning to think an institution might be best for Bobby and the only way to be fair to the other children. We hoped that we might be able to find a place more cheerful and less foreboding than the one we had already looked at. We didn't know what we were doing wrong, but Bobby was getting worse daily; perhaps someone else would know how to handle him.

At this point Louise's obstetrician/gynaecologist stepped in. The previous November at a Thanksgiving party he had seen the Sunshine Twins in action for the first time since their births – rampaging round his office, opening and emptying his drawers, while the other children quietly enjoyed watching the parade outside. Shortly after this he mentioned Dr Rachel Pinney, a British medical practitioner who had developed some new and unorthodox approaches to working with disturbed children. She had just arrived in New York, perhaps we would like to talk to her. He seemed to be careful not to raise our hopes unduly, and at that point Louise was fully occupied giving birth to Abigail, so we didn't pursue it immediately.

Later, however, he gave Louise Dr Pinney's telephone number and early in March Louise contacted her.

2 Rachel meets Bobby

Rachel in New York

When Bobby entered my life in the spring of 1977 I had been in New York for two months. I was sixty-seven; I had been frustrated in my efforts to do the work I wanted to do and was feeling let-down and depressed. There seemed no purpose in my being there at all. Looking back, I wonder – was I in New York to rescue Bobby? Or did he enter my life to rescue me?

I had arrived in New York the previous December, having chosen to come to the States because I had been invited to Los Angeles to demonstrate my work with children, but the November trip to Los Angeles had not been a success.

Early in 1977, an obstetrician acquaintance said to me more or less in passing, 'Would you take an autistic?'

My mind immediately rushed to the almost nothing that I knew about autistics – I had never been asked to deal with one at our clinic in Toronto. My friend Mollie Dundas had talked to me about her autistic unit at the Marlborough Day Hospital in London (which has now, alas, been closed); from her I had formed a vague concept that a child diagnosed as autistic was believed to have stopped developing socially at a certain age. At the unit, an army of voluntary aunties and uncles was recruited from the neighbourhood, and each would be instructed in treating a particular child as though it were still at the cut-off age, thus allowing it to go through the experience it had missed.

I had formed the mistaken notion that the aunties and uncles operated with the child outside the hospital unit. This was not in fact so: they operated within the closed walls of the centre only. I did not discover this until much later, and my ignorance of it probably helped when I let Bobby loose on the streets of New York.

I had acquired one other piece of information from Mollie: she had described to me how an autistic child who wants a door opened will take the hand of a nearby adult and place it on the door handle without relating to the adult as a person. These scraps constituted my entire knowledge of autism; no wonder I did not readily reply 'Of course' to the doctor's enquiry.

A month or so later he contacted me again. By this time I was depressed and disheartened; in fact I had started to pack my bags ready to go when he telephoned again. Bobby, he said, was the four-year-old son of a well-to-do couple whose third child he had recently delivered. The child was probably autistic, certainly unmanageable, and his parents' anxiety was doubled by the fact that his brother Billy, aged three, was beginning to copy Bobby's behaviour.

This time, without hesitation, I said, 'Yes'.

'Right, I'll give the mother your phone number.'

My heart sank, as I remembered the delays I had experienced in Canada. There was usually a month between a child's parents being given my number and their eventual call to make an appointment. In the case of a disturbed child whom I am to help, that lost month is agony. I believe that a month of Children's Hours at the age of four can prevent years of adult trouble, and it was in fact exactly one month later, at the beginning of March, that Bobby's mother phoned.

'Yes, I am Dr Pinney, yes I do accept kids with problems, no, I don't want to take a history yet.'

I did some hasty thinking. I was committed to return to Los Angeles in ten days' time; should I delay starting with this child until my return, or should I start now and make some arrangements to cover my absence? I thought of a child in Canada who had suffered greatly from a trip I had had to make to England shortly after starting his Children's Hours. Also I did not want at that moment to receive a child with bizarre behaviour in my present accommodation. Normally I would have seen Bobby alone where I live, so as to avoid being told his symptoms by his mother. So often I am told that a child is delinquent, aggressive, destructive, inattentive or possessing any of the other so-called behaviour disorders for which children get referred for treatment, but I rarely see any of this behaviour when I first meet the child, and am endeavouring to discover the well, whole personality behind the symptoms. This is best done in the absence of anxious parents who are, understandably, only too eager to describe what is wrong. Labels can be very destructive. Most people have heard the sort of de-personalizing conversation that goes on between members of hospital nursing staff: 'Has the double hernia had his lunch yet?' 'No, and while you're there, I've left my watch in Room Six – that's last week's colostomy.' It would be funny, if it weren't so hurtful to the patient.

All this was passing through my mind as I stood by the telephone, and I decided that I would see Bobby at once, in his own home, contrary to my usual practice. Agreeing to see Bobby initially with his mother was the first of what was to become a succession of breaks with my customary procedure. Every rule in the book was eventually to be discarded in the interests of Bobby's breakthrough – every rule, that is, except the basic principle of 'listen to the child, let him choose, let him grow'.

Meeting Bobby

Bobby's apartment was in a group of four skyscrapers surrounding a playground barred to traffic, with various subterranean glory-holes which he and I were to discover later. All this appeared to offer much of what a child needed, but I was soon to discover the significance of the omnipresent, brown-uniformed, truncheon-carrying security guards. Coming from England as I did, it was a long time before I realized their positive attributes; I was quick to discover their negative ones.

The door of the apartment did not open immediately: this was New York; where doors are not opened; elaborate chain systems operate to screen the callers, even if these are expected. Definite sounds were heard: children shouting, an adult shouting at the children to stop shouting, keys, locks, and other appliances going into action.

Eventually a small boy emerged like a bullet from a gun. Holding on to him was an anxious woman, evidently his mother, who was trying simultaneously to protest to Bobby that he couldn't go out, ask me to come in quickly, open the door enough to let me in, and prevent Bobby from getting out, and failing to do any of these things effectively – Bobby was 'mother-deaf'.

Somehow all of us were inside the flat and the door was double-locked, with an additional catch high up out of a child's reach. Surrounding me were Mother, Doreen, the large, black home help, and the two boys, Bobby and Billy.

As I squatted on the hall floor to get down to their level I said something to the child I thought was Bobby, and his mother, Louise, said quietly, 'That is Billy.' I felt rather ashamed of my mistake, and confused, since she had told me that Bobby was totally out of control while the only problem with Billy was that he was beginning to copy his brother. Their resemblance was accentuated by the fact that they were identically dressed in what appeared to be immaculate, expensive jeans and sweaters, which to me looked almost tailor-made. I asked his mother to put a belt on Bobby so that I could identify him, but as she put it on under his sweater that didn't help much.

However, I soon did begin to see a difference in their behaviour. Both were very interested in me, but as time went on I could see that Bobby's interest was caused by the presence of a new, strange body in his home, an object rather than a person. Billy, in contrast, competed fiercely for my attention, running round, talking non-stop and smiling a seductive smile. They were both almost constantly in motion.

The behaviour of the two boys was not an unusual experience; in general practice I had become accustomed to houses where the children were all over me while mother tried to restrain them and they took no notice. There was a difference in this household, however, that was hard to pinpoint straight away, my attention being pulled as it was in several directions at once.

It was difficult to tune in to the children without being rude to the mother, who was trying to make me feel at home by offering me coffee. Beside us, watching, stood the West Indian baby-sitter: full of nice, warm kindness, but distracting. I practise and preach single attention; another reason why I prefer to meet children without their parents. As I sat there, at the smart, polished table, I was not at ease, I hated myself, felt inadequate, accepted the inevitability of this, gritted my teeth, and got on with the routine, fact-finding mission known to doctors as 'taking a history'.

I asked Louise to write her answers to my initial questions, so that the boys would not hear themselves being discussed, while I used long words which they would not understand. Louise, at my request, kept the case history to a minimum – scarcely more than full name and date of birth.

I began then to notice a few things about my surroundings, and to realize what it was that had struck me as odd when I first arrived. There was an absence of lived-in untidiness; there were no toys around, though there were plenty of ornaments both hung on walls and placed on surfaces. In other households I have known with out-of-control children, the mother is always alert and anxious about the safety of the surrounding objects, backing her anxiety with remarks like 'Don't touch that!' and 'Mind you don't break that!', followed inevitably with 'Now look what you've done!' as a hanging plant falls to the floor.

The main activity of both small boys, meanwhile, was running rapidly up and down, at intervals coming to me, while completely ignoring their mother. Billy would try to attract my attention, while Bobby would stay around me for a while, aware of me though never looking directly at me, before running off again. Although I don't look for symptoms, of course I can see how a child is behaving, and Bobby's running was clearly not normal. He would trot a short way, as if with some intention, and then turn and trot back the same distance, up and down, up and down, flapping his hands in front of him in what is known as a stereotyped motion.

This meticulous sitting room, with its quantity of knick-knacks and carefully placed cushions, apparently needed no protection from two very mobile small children, one labelled as totally, and the other as partially, out of control. It was quite remarkable how safe all the grown-up objects were; it was remarkable, too, that Louise, clearly an anxious and insecure woman, seemed in no way worried about these objects. She seemed to have realized that Bobby simply did not break things.

When I said I wanted to use the lavatory, Louise preceded me and undid a shutting device high up on the door. My instinctive reaction – though I did not express it – was one of dismay that the bathroom should be latched from the outside with two small children in the flat. To me, to be locked out of a room that you have a right to be in is psychologically traumatic. However, I later learned that the boys had been helping themselves to their father's razor blades. I never discovered why these were not simply placed out of reach.

Bobby apparently shared my dislike of closed doors, for when I went in and tried to close this one, he was there immediately, ready with the weight of his body to transform the chink into an opening sizeable enough for him to get in.

His mother tried to stop him, without success; at no time during my visit did Bobby respond to her in any way. In my own place I wouldn't have hesitated to let Bobby view anything he wished, but here in a bathroom that was normally locked to him, and anxious to look respectable enough to be entrusted with the job of looking after him, I hesitated. Realizing that I was taking the risk of being labelled altogether too eccentric, I told Louise that I didn't mind using the lavatory with Bobby present. To my surprise, she left us together, Bobby standing almost on his head to watch me urinate.

When I came out, I asked to see the boys' room, and again Louise preceded me to undo the hooks outside, which were at adult level; every door and cupboard in the apartment had hooks on. The way these functioned was too complicated for me to understand. As far as I could make out, they were designed to protect the baby and to prevent casualties from falls out of a high window. Their effect, however, appeared to me to be unnecessary restriction of the boys' freedom.

The boys' room was very clean and tidy, and rather stark. The first thing to strike me was the curtainless window which had heavy mesh fixed across it, presumably to prevent climbing boys from falling out. If there were any toys, they had been tidied away.

When we returned to the living room, Louise brought up the subject of Billy.

'He wants to go to school,' she said, 'But he knows he can't while he is still wearing nappies.'

I must have given a questioning look, because she added guiltily, 'They are both in nappies.'

I was surprised; I could not associate nappies with those dark-blue, tight-fitting, belted jeans; where was the bulk with which I was familiar from my own children and grandchildren in England? I had forgotten that this was America in the 1970s, with its slimline, disposable nappies. Also I was concerned that Bobby's and Billy's genitals must have been pressed up tight against their trousers all day, with no access to hand, sight or toilet. The kind of damage this must have done is commonplace knowledge in these post-Freudian days.

Poor Louise, with her guilt and anxiety, must have gone through agony in telling me all this; I now feel sad that I failed to respond to her obvious need. When she admitted that she had breast-fed none of her three babies, however, she showed no guilt at all. On the issue of breast-feeding, USA 1977 would have been on her side, whereas in the matter of nappies she was offending her culture norm. From the viewpoint of damage to Bobby, the absence of breast-feeding was probably a far greater deprivation than being made to shit in his pants.

Louise was deeply uncertain of herself as a person and as a mother. She had no instinct for child rearing: she was unable to handle her children with physical affection, as I saw later when she was with the baby; if she loved her children, she was unable to show them that she did. With no one to turn to for help, she had set about doing to perfection the things that she *could* do: dressing the children immaculately and keeping the apartment tidy and clean.

It occurred to me that Bobby's mother was as tightly locked in to trying to live up to her image of good wife in a well furnished flat as Bobby was in his prison of non-communication. I had already noticed that Bobby made no demands on his mother; there was none of the mother-pestering usual with a disturbed child of that age. It was as if he had given up trying to get what he needed from her. Mother and Bobby struck me as two prisoners, each needing to lean on the other, neither of them able to do so; each of them compromising by respecting the other's privacy.

But my services were accepted. I was to see Bobby next day and settle finance with his father the day after that. The adventure had begun.

3 Bobby meets Rachel

Bobby's life before I met him

One of the most striking things about Bobby when I first met him was his apparent lack of resentment of his prison. He seems to have reacted to it as I saw him react to all the limits which he found himself up against later. He gave his excellent brain a full-time job finding out what the limits were, and spent some of his energies in trying to find ways of extending them. The rest of his energies he spent in learning all that he could, in the minutest detail, of what was accessible to him within his confines. He seemed to have none left over with which to be angry about his situation. And yet, of course, the frustration and anger must have been there.

It is true that on the rare occasions when he met other children Bobby behaved aggressively towards them. The neighbours knew him as 'that boy who bites and kicks other kids – they shouldn't allow him in the playground' – 'that boy who's totally out of control – they should have him seen to!'

Most of the time Bobby stayed inside the apartment, where he had the television, a few toys with which he seldom played, the view of the streets through the mesh across his window, and his brother Billy. Occasionally he was taken out, either locked into his pushchair or held in an iron grip by the home help, Doreen, who also somehow managed to get him fed, undressed and to bed.

The picture of Bobby as a prisoner was enhanced for me by the security guards; a whole team of them in formidable brown uniforms, who patrolled the apartment block where he lived. They were considered a necessity by the residents and no doubt, in New York, they were. But did they have to spend so much time in Bobby-prevention? One of their regular tasks apparently was to prevent Bobby from 'escaping', from being in a lift alone, from finding out about revolving doors, from exploring basements and other children's glory-holes; from indulging, in fact, in anything and everything he needed to do in order to grow and learn. They carried truncheons and walkie-talkies on which they could inform each other when Bobby 'got loose'.

To the security guards Bobby was an established hazard of daily life, that crazy kid who mustn't be allowed to escape, because everyone knew that if he did there was no ordinary way of retrieving him since he didn't respond to calling. As there was no way Bobby could or would relate to them, and no way that they could relate to him, there was simply a war situation. He was treated with all the precautions that might be expected had a wild animal taken up residence in the block.

My overall picture of Bobby when I met him was that of a prisoner with an enormous urge to escape; a classification well-known in adult jails. He thought hard all day: how to learn the limited environment he had, and how to get out of it. His father once said to me, 'If there is a way, Bobby will find it.'

'You won't fall, Bobby!'

At 11 a.m. next day I stood in the foyer of my block, alert and ready for any emergency. I had no anxiety about Bobby himself; whatever his behaviour, no matter how bizarre or unpredictable, I felt sure I could handle it. The anxieties I did have were as to whether I could handle the public.

Bobby announced his arrival by lifting the intercom telephone outside the front door, which had the effect of buzzing the reception desk. Through the glass front door I could see his mother making frantic and vain efforts to stop him, and, once inside, he immediately shot like a rabbit through some private doors to the right. Louise threw me his coat; I caught it, saying rapidly, 'Come back in fifty minutes,' and shot through the doors after him.

Once through, there was no sign of him. During the following nine months I never did succeed in arriving at a door in time to see where Bobby had disappeared to on the other side. It was as if there was an automatic shut-off which operated when the first door closed behind him, rendering him invisible until he was safely through another door. I soon learned to abandon the direct method of trying to keep Bobby in sight; it just didn't work. I would go through the last door he was seen to go through and then switch on my Bobby-tuned antennae, which I had plenty of opportunity to develop as time went on.

The doors through which Bobby darted on that first occasion, and on many future occasions, led to a catering establishment which rented some ground-floor space in the apartment block. I never discovered exactly what they did there, but I used to see a seemingly-endless stream of butcher-clothed, strong young men coming through those swing doors carrying large platters of various sorts of meat joints. As the doors swung both ways I soon saw just how dangerous a darting Bobby, approximately thigh high, could be to those meat-platter-carrying young giants. At this early stage it would have been totally useless to try to explain a thing like this to Bobby; in no way would he have heard me. It was to be some time before I would be able to get his attention to make any sort of communication involving danger.

Having failed to locate Bobby inside the catering establishment, I went back into the foyer and waited for him to come out in his own time, which he did, unaccompanied moreover by any irate caterer. Throughout my time with Bobby, that catering establishment, which had plenty to put up with, continued to be friendly and co-operative. I took Bobby to the lift, and as we proceeded up to my apartment I

gave him my customary speech of admission to an Hour. I
cannot remember exactly what words I used, but at some
level he understood it and I knew that he had understood it.

We entered my one-room and bathroom apartment. Since
I had not got things going in New York the room was barely
equipped with play material, and I was slightly uncomfortable about this. Bobby's lack of interest in play material,
however, was total. He took in the scene as it affected him.

He saw a large window wide open at the bottom; right up
against the window was my bed. Bobby leaped on to the bed
and lay full length on his stomach with his head as far out as
he could get it, while keeping his centre of gravity on the bed
side of the window. He surveyed the scene below from five
storeys up, and was happy.

As he leaned out of the window, he mumbled, 'Bob . . .
'all.' For the first time, I understood his speech.

I replied, 'You *won't* fall, Bobby.'

Bobby heard, and continued leaning out.

This direct contradiction of what he had said is an
example of the many times I had to break the basic
Children's Hours method in order to adapt it to Bobby's
special needs.

This exchange, sometimes vocal, sometimes just understood with the trust that developed between us, was to be
repeated regularly over a period of a month or so, but I shall
never forget the look on Bobby's face that first day when I
told him he wouldn't fall. This was Bobby, who was 'deaf' to
incoming voices. His realization that I understood was
established, and has remained established to this day.

I was soon to acquire a whole team of Bobby helpers, and
many of them simply could not take the situation of Bobby
leaning out of a fifth-floor window. We had frequent talks
about it; my advice to them was to ensure that the window
was shut before they entered the flat or, failing that, to make
sure that the bed was pulled away from the window. Having
done this, they should tell Bobby that this was because they,

the adults, were afraid of heights, taking the responsibility fairly on their own shoulders while assuring Bobby that they knew *he* was all right.

And he was all right. What idiots we are to try to tell children where their centre of gravity is! 'Be careful!' we tell them. 'You'll fall!' What chance have young children, who know perfectly well where their centre of gravity is, of maintaining balance against the barrage of 'Be carefuls' issued by adults?

On one occasion I have to admit that even I felt distinctly queasy. This time Bobby lay on the bed and swung his legs round till they were out of the window from approximately the knees downwards. What I did was to break my own rules by appearing to initiate a communication.

'You won't fall, Bobby,' I said, sitting in a friendly position near him on the bed, being careful not to touch him or look in any way as if I was guarding him. Again, Bobby heard, and shortly afterwards found the view uninteresting and changed his position.

After he had had his fill of the window, Bobby began to explore objects, mumbling to himself. I recapped his actions, though I couldn't catch most of his words. 'Now you're holding the clock . . . Now you're looking at the tape recorder . . . It's best not to put your hands on this bit of the tape recorder, because it might break, and I wouldn't like it to get broken . . . Now you're going in the bathroom . . . Now you've opened the cupboard . . . Oh, that's a cookie is it? . . . Now you're eating the cookie.'

This recapping looks odd to grown-ups, but to the child it conveys clearly that he has your full attention and approval, whatever he says or does, unrestricted by adult values.

Rachel meets Bobby's father
I gave Bobby his second Hour next day, a Sunday, and in the afternoon met his father.

We had arranged to meet at a café not far from where I

lived. Robert Senior turned out to be a good-looking man in his forties, smartly dressed in the sort of clothes worn by successful American businessmen; he was well-mannered and charming.

One of the first things Robert Senior told me was that Bobby was gifted with a remarkable intelligence. I believe that some IQ tests had been done, but of course these are difficult to carry out on a non-talking child. Nevertheless, Robert was convinced of it, and talked with pride of Bobby's phenomenal memory, one evidence of which was his knowledge of television. Bobby knew every programme in detail, every actor, announcer and channel.

His father, I think, never really accepted the link between this very high intelligence and Bobby's unmanageable behaviour. It was a new phenomenon to me, too.

A highly intelligent child finds himself in an environment whose values are based on a very much lower average intelligence; he senses a difference between himself and the outside world and he has not the knowledge, the experience or the means to express his feeling that his own values are right in comparison with the environment's much lower standard of values. He is more sensitive, more thin-skinned than the average child who just accepts the world as it is, and he is made aware very early on that he is 'different'.

My concept of an autistic child in the category to which Bobby belongs is one who is born with a very exceptional amount of *something*; it is not intellect alone; perhaps you could call it intellect-plus. He opens his eyes, looks at the world and says, 'Is this what I'm expected to relate to? No, thank you!' And he shuts his eyes again and keeps them shut.

It became clear to me, during this meeting and later on, that Bobby's father valued pure intellect very highly, and so valued Bobby. He had pride in having such a brilliant son, and distress that the son could not be educated. Every one of the doctors and educationalists he had visited had, he said, been less helpful than the last; Bobby was probably headed for an institution when he found our non-directive, non-evaluative and fully attentive method.

It is to Robert Senior's credit that he allowed me to pursue this method with his son, for it was quite contrary to his own philosophy. He had not learned that the way to relate to Bobby was to relate to him exactly where he was at any particular moment, and not try to divert his attention to a subject of Father's choice. He still shared the widespread belief that education is the imparting of knowledge; I don't, I believe that education is having experiences. Like many other fathers, he pictured himself as the wise man whose duty and pleasure it was to place the maximum opportunity for acquiring knowledge in the path of his son. He denied that he was educationally pressuring; he said that he just exposed the child to knowledge.

During our time together I have observed Robert on many occasions drawing Bobby's attention to what he as an adult considers to be suitable educational material. For example, Bobby will be in a car with one hundred per cent concentration on the environment of his choice – street signs, buses, roads and so on. Father will attempt to distract his attention in order to point out a building or other object of historical value. Bobby has, as far as I have been able to observe, no sense of history at all. If ever I have seen anyone live totally in the present, it is Bobby.

Robert Senior prided himself on his quiet, logical, detached attitude. I never saw him angry; he continued to try to be reasonable and logical with his son, but failed to pitch that logic and reasoning at Bobby's level.

As for his relationships with people, Robert Senior confirmed that Billy was the only person with whom Bobby could communicate, although at that stage Bobby did not see his brother as a real person. Billy could understand Bobby's garbled language, when no one else could. Most of their games consisted of Bobby telling Billy what to do, and Billy either doing it or fighting back. Otherwise, Bobby had no kind of relationship with anyone, and no one could get him to do anything other than what he wanted to do, although Louise had succeeded in getting him dressed and to remain dressed, after a phase during which he had had to be sewn into his clothes.

There is one factor in my relationship with Bobby's father which must be stated: I do not cease to be grateful for the trust he placed in me that day and did not withdraw later. It must have been strained quite severely at times; for example when I would produce new assistants and blandly announce that I had hired them in the street the day before. Robert would accept such statements with no signs of wavering in his trust, although his attitudes to such matters were very different from mine. Without that trust, I could never have done what I did, and Bobby would never have made his breakthrough.

Here is Robert's own account of that first meeting.

Robert meets Rachel (by Robert)
In the past year we'd heard a lot of precise, scientific-sounding labels attached to Bobby: autism, developmental aphasia, minimum brain dysfunction. Those doctors who struck me as intellectually honest, though, had pointed out that such labels are merely rough descriptive terms for certain kinds of behaviour.

Unfortunately none of these labels stood for known causes or effective cures. The only agreement among the doctors was that Bobby's condition was organic in nature but not traumatic in origin; and that no physical anomaly, such as brain damage, was indicated.

After her meeting with Rachel, Louise filled me in on the 'Children's Hours' concept as she understood it. Rachel hadn't offered any theoretical explanation, but her approach obviously differed from all the others we'd heard about. Instead of applying outside forces in an attempt to modify Bobby's behaviour, she proposed, in some way I didn't understand and perhaps she didn't either, to free forces inside Bobby which would enable him to do the job himself.

I liked that idea. It was similar to the basic principle of aeronautical design: the plane flies itself; that is, a well-designed airplane will fly straight and level in the air even with the pilot's hands off the controls. Maybe Rachel could help Bobby achieve this stability as a person.

I was not overly concerned whether Rachel's methodology had been 'officially' validated by the medical establishment. Not that I regard 'orthodox medicine' as a term of opprobrium. On the contrary; if the practice of medicine is an art and not a science, the art still must have a base of accurate knowledge, i.e. science. But this area was, by their own admission, all but *terra incognita* to the medical mainstreamers, and maybe this maverick British doctor was on to something.

Louise's reaction to Rachel had been positive. Although she felt intimidated and almost overwhelmed by this forceful, sixty-seven-year-old high-energy Englishwoman, she had the instinctive feeling that this was the right direction for Bobby. On the other hand, Louise was absolutely at the end of her rope, and her impulsive trust might, in Dr Johnson's phrase, represent the triumph of hope over experience.

I arranged to meet Rachel at midday on Sunday 6 March, in the lobby of her building. (By now, even before meeting her, I was calling her 'Rachel' because she had insisted that Louise do so.)

I knew what to expect from Louise's description. Rachel was certainly distinctive in appearance: short and tubby, her untidy grey hair cut to minimum length for a woman. She wore baggy slacks, and a baggy sweater over several other layers. The term 'British physician' may imply Harley Street, honed skills and ineffable silkiness of manner, but Rachel was, at least in appearance, at the other end of that spectrum.

It was 'Rachel' and 'Robert' from the start. She told me

some of her background and elaborated on Children's Hours, making it clear that her approach was not like any of those currently pursued by establishment doctors. This wasn't a plus to me, but neither was it a minus, inasmuch as the orthodox approaches weren't working.

Bobby's problems, she said, arose from the fact that his emotional development had stopped at the infant stage. His superior intelligence was of no help in getting his growth going again, but rather was probably at least one of the factors responsible for it having stopped in the first place.

What had to be done, Rachel continued, was to go back with him to that earlier state, and give him an environment in which he could resume his progress. It might be necessary to regress him to an even earlier point so that he could 're-do' the developmental stages where things had gone wrong. If this were necessary – and Rachel was almost sure it would be – the parents should realize that in some ways his behaviour would appear 'worse' as he struggled to resume his progress.

Rachel proposed a six-month programme in which she and her staff would work with Bobby and, to a lesser extent, with Billy. Part of the programme would involve taking Bobby out of the home environment, preferably away from the New York area, for extended periods.

As she crisply laid out her plan, I was becoming convinced by Rachel's self-confidence, compassion and forthrightness. The approach felt 'right' to me.

But I didn't come totally around to her side until she suddenly lost her assertiveness when she had to raise the necessary subject: money. The self-confidence ebbed out of her as she moved from the details of her work to the financial side of her proposal, which she laid out awkwardly, fiddling with the tea things on the formica table, glancing down as if she'd just confessed some grievous sin.

I was taken aback at this lapse from the doctor-patient psychodrama. The physicians I had previously dealt with would have shifted from medicine to money with the inexorable smoothness of the Cadillacs they drove – was Rachel a *real* doctor?

This was the moment Rachel came into sharp focus for me: she *was* a real doctor, her attention fixed on the needs of the patient, and the business relationship so irrelevant as to be embarrassing to her. I thought of the verse from St Matthew: 'Lay not up for yourself treasures on earth, where moth and dust doth corrupt, and thieves break in and steal; but store up for yourself treasures in heaven, for where your treasure is, there also is your heart.' Rachel was the first physician I ever knew who exemplified this ideal; and from that instant my confidence in her has never wavered.

I did not haggle over the flat amount she named. To me it was large; I didn't have it and would have to borrow it. But it was modest in comparison to what any American doctor would have charged, and out of it Rachel would pay her staff and all expenses for the travelling with Bobby which she planned.

The borrowing, though, would exhaust my credit capacity. If further funds were required, I didn't know where they'd come from, and I tried to make this point to Rachel. She had dealt herself out of the money economy so completely that she regarded those of us who remained in it as uniformly 'rich'. She had a lilies-of-the-field attitude towards her own needs, which, whatever they turned out to be, could be met by my limitless resources.

Possibly anaesthetized by the strain of talking money, she did not grasp the whole of what I was saying, but we agreed on the basic amount; and in all our dealings after that I found her accommodating and generous.

4 We Begin

A child's first language is play; he may use play-language, verbal or physical, to act out all kinds of inner conflicts. It is not the Hour-taker's role to interpret these; the adult's role is to *receive* what the child is doing, not to understand it. Of course, some moments are so dramatic that one cannot help interpreting them; many such moments were to occur with Bobby; however, the taker never allows interpretation to interfere with the Hour.

Sometimes, DDI* limits must be brought into action, as when Bobby wanted to touch my tape recorder head; but this is never done with a direct 'No' or any sense of disapproval. Another occasion was when he put his hand straight on the hot-plate of the cooker without looking first to see whether it was hot. It wasn't, because this is the kind of danger you should check before the child arrives, but I said, in a very gentle voice – and again without an outright 'No' – 'Watch it, be careful, it might be hot.' By the end of that first week, Bobby would check for himself before touching the hot-plate. I found that he accepted limits surprisingly well.

There was no sign from Bobby that he could hear my recapping, but I sensed that he did. I was impressed by the care and control with which he handled objects, and his constant search for new experiences. One helper, knowing nothing of autism, made the interesting remark afterwards that, as he ran round picking up this and picking up that, he seemed 'hungry', not for food but for some fulfilment, some form of satisfaction; she added that he seemed to

* Danger, damage and impropriety

have trouble relating to people and so related to objects instead.

Unlike some conventional forms of child therapy, Children's Hours are not restricted to the playroom. If the child wants to go outside during an Hour, then he goes out, followed by the taker. Bobby's biggest desire in those early days was to get outside and explore. My front door was easy enough to open, and having seen all he wanted to see inside, Bobby opened it. He proceeded outside, closely followed by a helper and myself, still recapping his actions: 'I see, you're going out now . . . I see, you're going along the corridor . . . You want to go this way . . . We're going down the stairs, are we?'

Alterations to the building had left several short staircases which were blocked off by a flat wooden partition. One of these blind-alley staircases immediately became a happy hunting ground for Bobby, and he was to spend much of his first ten days on it. The stairs were flanked on one side by a wall and on the other side by an ornate railing. Bobby spent much time going up and down this stairway, touching the patterns on the railings; the shapes clearly meant something to him, for he would murmur, 'This is a brush, this is a . . .'. I never did discover what the second object was; Bobby's articulation of his almost non-language was at that time nearly impossible to understand. It was nonetheless very real and full of meaning to him, and it was not important for me to understand it. What was important was for me to convey to Bobby that he had my full attention.

Although he did not communicate directly with us, he had understood straight away what an Hour was about, and now he directed the helper and me to go up and down the stairs, knowing that we were 'with' him. He moved as always at top speed, often slipping, his movements jerky, as though he wanted to be in control of himself but didn't quite know how. Very often he uttered the word 'up' when he meant 'down'; in that case I recapped what he meant, not what he said. The decision to do this is still widely discussed within our team. I am myself not sure yet whether the word or the presumed exact opposite thought should be recapped.

At the end of Bobby's Hour the helper and I discussed what had gone on. She said, 'At first, when you were explaining to me about the Hour, I thought it was a very good idea, but that perhaps children need more direction. After seeing the Hour – I was wrong!'

She also commented, rightly I thought, that she felt Bobby had anger inside him, which was not being expressed. When he did, how would I handle it? I told her, 'In an Hour it's no problem at all – he just expresses it and you take it. The biggest problem is the parents, because when they start to see him getting better and expressing his anger they may think he's getting worse and take him away.'

I began to realize during this discussion how important it is to involve the parents. This is always difficult; I know that many people these days do family therapy; I do not: my personal talent is with children up to about eleven. If necessary I will suggest that the parents see another counsellor, but the child's Hour is always private to the child; to let parents see or tell them what goes on in it would immediately negate the freedom of that Hour. Of course, parents are curious, and some get worried. In Toronto they used to come to me saying, 'What the hell goes on in there? All I ever hear is that he eats peanut butter!'

I decided at that moment that I would try to let both parents sit in on an Hour with somebody else's child; I never managed to do this with Louise, but it was not long before Robert was able not only to observe an Hour but to take one himself.

Because of my firm commitment to visit Los Angeles, I decided to fit in as many sessions with Bobby as I could before I left, so as to give him the security that there was more to come when I returned; and do the best I could for him by providing other helpers while I was away. They would attend Bobby's Hours as observers while I was there and take him out as often as possible during my absence. One of these people was Eileen, who came to observe several times. There was to have been another helper, but unfortunately she had to drop out.

So, with Eileen learning, pencil and paper at the ready, Bobby's Hours got under way. And it was not long before my little team had its first taste of the public's reactions to Bobby.

I was now living in a former hotel, an old building with wide corridors. It was here that I first experienced Bobby's impact on the outside world.

Bobby was fascinated by switches of every sort; in fact he was fascinated by everything pertaining to twentieth-century technology. When out and free he acted firmly on the principle of 'Press the button first, ask questions afterwards'. The button-pushing would start on our way up in the lift, where his fascination with buttons was intensified by his fascination with numbers. He would indicate that he wanted me to lift him up so that he could reach the button-panel, and sometimes all the buttons within reach would be pushed.

If there were other people in the lift there would be complaints, to which Bobby was deaf but I was not. I found myself in a dilemma: I would try to be my usual polite Rachel who is perfectly happy to let other people have their way, but at the same time I wanted to make sure that Bobby had *his* way. I got round it by smiling sweetly at people who found themselves going up when they wanted to go down, and explaining that Bobby was a rather special child. All my neighbours got to know him in the end; there were two lifts, so anyone with Bobby phobia would quickly get into the other one when they saw us coming.

Once we got to my flat there was the ordinary light switch, the switch in the walk-in closet and a switch in the bathroom. All these were tried out by Bobby before he moved on to the telephone, both the one on my desk and the intercom phone inside the closet, which buzzed the reception desk. The reception desk staff were naturally irritated by this, and after a while I would warn them when I was giving an Hour so that they could ignore it. Finally, there was a digital clock, cylindrical in shape, which had a lot of buttons to press and turn; this absorbed Bobby daily. He would turn the knobs and change the numbers, sometimes making garbled, unintelligible comments.

Once he had tried out every available switch in my flat – ignoring what play material there was, to my continued surprise – and looked into the bathroom without trying any water play, there was not much to keep Bobby inside my flat. So out we went, followed by whoever was observing.

We started to have neighbour trouble almost straightaway. Bobby was not making a lot of noise, but he would run up and down the corridors, sometimes jabbering in excitement, delighting in his freedom. But there is something about the sound of running that alarms people; it upsets them to see or hear children run. It is also a sad fact that some people are irritated by the shouting of a happy child. One of the reasons for this is that the child's cries remind adults at an unconscious level of the times when they were children and were made to shut up by the attending adults; unconsciously they replay the situation that was imposed on them.

Hearing running footsteps and happy cries, folk would appear at their apartment doors and tell Bobby he was making too much noise. I would stay supportively with him giving him non-verbal reassurance that what he was doing was all right; he had a right to be there and a right to make a reasonable amount of noise. I couldn't say this aloud – Bobby wouldn't have understood my words, and it would only have increased the neighbours' hostility; but I could feel it, act it, and behave in such a way that Bobby could pick up what I meant, which he was quick to do.

At the same time, with Bobby's unspoken permission, I

would explain to the neighbours as carefully as I could that this was a deprived child who had not had the opportunity of playing before; please would they accept him and help me to get him better? I said nothing that would identify Bobby's parents or lay blame on them; in fact I found that without telling a downright lie people's sympathies were more easily engaged if they got the impression that he had been in an institution. My explanations were necessarily brief, because by this time Bobby would have shot off elsewhere and I would have to follow, but the effect of my communications was to defuse hostility in some cases, and gain allies in others. I began to make a note of the apartment numbers of friendly neighbours, and of ones to avoid at all costs – the men, I found, were usually more tolerant than the women.

One particularly unfriendly woman used to wait for us to be on the stairs and then open her door and start abusing us. She was the sort of person whom no amount of soft-soaping by me would have mellowed, although I tried. Bobby would ignore her up to a point, but beyond that point he would scream, spit and run away. The irate flat-owner would then feel totally justified in her opinion of the child as unruly, spiteful and out of control.

Had Bobby been communicable-with, I would have made a rule of 'No spitting outside the playroom', as I had done with one of the children in Canada, but at this stage there was no way I could get him to understand such a rule. When provoked, Bobby spat. And there was no way that I could convey to the people spat at that if they had not first given offence to the child, the child would not have given offence to them. One of my basic principles is to be extra polite to children. If you are polite to the child, he will be polite to you; but it is the adult who has the power and ability to start the dialogue of politeness.

Bobby explored the outside world with vigour. The handle of every closed door was a challenge; he turned them all, and if he found one unlocked he would go through the doorway. A housewife would be peacefully minding her own business, when suddenly her front door would open and a very mobile small person with a remote look in his eyes would come running in and quickly go round the apartment checking out all doors, switches and mechanical objects, followed by Rachel and her assistant five feet behind. The average tenant would find this somewhat unnerving, and her reaction was understandable, to put it mildly.

'Hey! What do you think you're doing? Get out of here!'

While I was giving a speedy explanation and apology, Bobby would run swiftly out to another part of the building, turning on and off all switches within his sight and reach, and often arousing anger in the people who were affected. Undaunted, he would increase the pace of his investigations. At this stage some adult might start in pursuit: Bobby would run faster, pressing more and more buttons and door-bells, showing amazing skill in avoiding damage in the process.

I do not advocate giving freedom to children to run wild the whole time. A child who is given an Hour understands and accepts that the rules are different during the other twenty-three. Of course children need guidance; they must be shown or told (politely) when objects are dangerous or easily damaged, and it should if necessary be explained to them that people may not like the way they are behaving. In the case of the hitherto imprisoned Bobby, however, it was important to allow him to go where he wanted to during his Hours. It was also important that the neighbours shouldn't be annoyed too much. I was always putting these two things on the weighing machine: the price that the neighbours paid against the value of freedom to Bobby; and sometimes I would stop him and sometimes I wouldn't.

Some of the neighbours became friends to us both. There was a woman on the top floor: I first saw her standing forlornly outside her door; she had lost her cat and was very upset about it. Bobby made a bee-line into her flat, and she let him go round, checking everything out; perhaps she welcomed the distraction. We visited her quite a lot and she became a good friend. She was a trombone-player, and later on she once let Bobby play the trombone – very carefully, because if you bend a trombone, the trombone has had it. I used to visit her on my own, too.

On one occasion, also later on, Bobby knocked on the door of an apartment shared by a drummer and his girlfriend. When the girlfriend opened it he slipped under her arm, which was his usual way of effecting an entry, and rushed straight for the drums. I was terrified he would hurt the drums and followed him quickly in to protect them. But the drummer said, 'No, he's all right, let him be, let him play the drum.' I thought it was marvellous that the drummer should tell *me* to let him be! Bobby loved the drummer. He visited the apartment over and over again to play the drums, and always received a warm welcome.

After a few days Bobby was much more relaxed and at ease, and accepted that there were apartments he must not go into. Getting him to go home, however, was always difficult. He never wanted to go; he would run away if he could, and would have to be caught and removed bodily, yelling and struggling. When his mother or Doreen came to collect him, I would take Bobby down to the foyer and beat a retreat as quickly as possible, rather than aggravate the situation by joining in the hassle. Sometimes Bobby managed to slip away and was back again in my flat before I reached it, and I would have to bring him down all over again.

My departure for L.A. was looming nearer, but Bobby was becoming daily easier to handle and I was confident that Eileen would do a good job in my absence.

When I told Louise that there would only be one helper, Eileen, she was very concerned, partly because Robert was going to be away the same week as I was, also in Los Angeles, and she was going to be in a real mess on her own with the two boys. But chiefly because she had already seen a subtle change in Bobby; she knew that having Hours was making him happy, and she was worried, as I was, that he would feel let down when these suddenly came to a stop.

I thought the best thing would be to arrange for a team of helpers to take him out every day, as opposed to giving him Hours. I felt he would not be too difficult to handle; he was so used to being told that he couldn't do things that when he was allowed to do most of the things he wanted, he accepted necessary limits quite easily. Eileen was willing to help, and had quickly caught on to my methods. I hastily searched for other assistants; I found one or two young people who were willing to try, and sent them out on some experimental outings with Eileen but without me.

These went well. Eileen and the others reported that at first it was difficult to get Bobby out of his apartment; he wanted to come but seemed to need permission. Billy wanted to come too, and tried to follow, which made Bobby very angry. Once out, however, he seemed very happy, although, as one of them said, 'He seemed to have to *do* something. He was very intent on always moving, as though he were going away for something, but at the same time looking for some-thing.'

They spent most of the time in the lifts of Bobby's block, with Bobby selecting the floors at which he would get out, running a few feet, and then getting back in. He seemed at his happiest inside the lift, though one of the observers, a young actor, noticed the almost adult seriousness of his face when he first got in and looked at the numbers, his eyebrows pulled down and his lips stiff and tense. Bobby's tension relaxed as the Hour continued, but when he sensed that it would be time to go home he became increasingly nervous, pushing all the lift buttons except the one to his home.

As they finally took him up to his own floor, he appeared frightened, his voice shaking as he counted, 'One, two, three'; he seemed, the actor said, to be holding on to the numbers for security. Eileen had to pick him up and carry him to his apartment; outside the door he declared in his own language, but quite understandably, that he was really sick and needed a doctor! The first time they took him back he had a tantrum when his mother opened the door; on the second occasion however, he just shot inside, with no time for goodbyes to be said.

I was fascinated to hear their comments; I was beginning to feel that Bobby might benefit from having a whole-day babysitter as well as Hours. Ideally, I would have liked to organize one while I was away; as it was, I arranged a rota of helpers to take him out every day.

Just a week after he met me, and before my departure, Bobby met my roof. All that week he had been fascinated by the lift buttons in my block which went from B to 13, followed by the mysterious letters 'PH' at the top. Bobby tested out 'PH' several times; it was non-functional; he also uttered the letters, although as his language was almost incomprehensible I simply received what he was saying and did not at first connect his words with lift-buttons.

Then one day, while exploring the thirteenth floor, Bobby found some steps and went up them; at the top was a door fastened shut with the flimsiest of catches. I had no idea where it led to and was a little reluctant to open the catch and allow Bobby to project himself into the unknown. That did not stop me from opening it.

We emerged into fairyland. Even my mature, nearly seventy-year-old soul responded to unexpected fairyland.

PH was the fourteenth floor and the magical letters stood for Penthouse. There before us was a large roof with various barriers breaking it up into segments and areas, each with its own individual character and private magical aura. Round the edges were small sheds, some locked, some open, some smelling of emptiness and some containing stored – mostly junk–furniture, with a different but equally fascinating smell.

Coming out into this magic place Bobby immediately assessed its boundaries. Around the edge of the flat roof was a balustrade which was about breast-high to him. It was this balustrade with its view of the streets far below that mostly captivated Bobby's sense of wonder: here he was, with no window barrier between him and the streets below.

Bobby bolted towards the balustrade like a rabbit under gunfire. He always got from A to B as quickly as possible, allowing no delay between decision and action. At home he had been surrounded by loving and caring adults, but no way had their loving and caring made Bobby regard them as other than impediments to his freedom.

I was able to let Bobby loose; I was not a parent, I was a professional; I looked for no return from Bobby other than the opportunity to observe his emergence into life and freedom. I was able to calculate and take risks that a parent would have found emotionally impossible – not that I did not occasionally find them difficult myself. This episode of his first exit on to the roof was one of those occasions.

As Bobby, at full speed, approached the low wall at the side of the roof, I felt sick; I am by no means good at heights. I calculated quickly: if I ran behind him, he would hear me and run faster, and perhaps his judgement would be impaired when he reached the wall. Having decided I must not be observed to be running behind him, I cheated somewhat, and ran quietly, ready to switch to a nonchalant walk if he turned round. My running while not appearing to run is not behaviour I would teach or recommend to others; it is cheating; it is simply what I did then because I am a fallible human.

As I ran, unobserved, I quickly became realistic about any action I could or should take if I arrived at the balustrade at the same time as Bobby. I realized that the only really helpful thing that I could offer him was my calm acceptance of his safety. He had no suicidal intentions; he just wanted to see what life below looked like from my roof fourteen floors above Broadway. As my reasoning took charge, my nausea somewhat left me; I walked fast, as casually as I could, and arrived at the edge shortly after Bobby. He had jumped up so that he was lying with his tummy on the wall and his head over the edge.

I used the orthodox language of Children's Hours and recapped his actions: 'You are now lying on the wall, and can see the street below.'

My sickness had become minimal; it only returned slightly when I myself looked at the street below, and was somewhat lessened by my paying attention to the down-below scene as it looked to Bobby. But I could not totally lose my fear – that kind of fear has deep roots, although I personally have never come across it in a small child.

That was the first of many happy sessions which Bobby and I spent on the roof; it was a most explorable place, a paradise for any child, with its numerous sheds, some locked, some open, and all of interest to Bobby. There was much evidence of human activity in the shape of paintpots, newly stored articles and carpentry, but the fate that had on so many occasions failed to look after Bobby's interests made up for the failure in good measure when it came to the magical PH: not once did we encounter a workman or any potentially dangerous adult ('dangerous', in Bobby's terms, meaning Bobby-activity-frustrating), or in fact any adult employed by or connected with the management. Fate was certainly on Bobby's side there, protecting his emergence from the chrysalis via the enchanted PH.

I was as delighted by PH as was Bobby, though perhaps for different reasons. There, I was free from the public. These were early days, and I had yet to encounter the full force of public opposition to Bobby-activity in such places as buses, trains, streets and shops; I had, however, had a taste of what was to come in the lifts, corridors and reception foyer; I had had enough of a taste to realize what tremendously hard work it was to be 'with' Bobby and to deal appropriately with the public at the same time. On that roof, I could give my whole attention to being with Bobby.

For many happy weeks most of Bobby's Hours were spent on PH, with me sharing its magic with him. Bobby, the roof, myself, my many helpers, a New York spring, the total absence of outside interference, all together make that roof one of the beauty spots in my memory of those times.

The day before I left, Billy came for his first Hour and I was able to see more clearly the difference between him and Bobby. Billy behaved like an ordinary little boy; there was no difficulty in leaving mother, no raised eyebrows from the staff and public in the foyer, no anxiety over button-pushing in the lift. In fact, there was nothing to single out the Rachel/Billy unit as peculiar in any way, except for the greetings of a few people who had already met me with Bobby, whose expressions indicated, 'Is this the same child? No, not possible.'

So an ordinary child took an ordinary leave of an ordinary parent and progressed in an orderly way in an orderly lift to my room. Having been told that he could do just what he liked, except anything *really* bad, Billy gave a quick look round the room, played perfunctorily with the cooker, opened and closed the fridge door and did some cursory play with some wooden blocks before finally settling for the bath-room. Here he turned on the taps, eagerly removed his clothes and got into the bath, taking with him various plastic containers, blocks, toy animals – in fact all the usual objects to be found in a young-child-inhabited bathroom.

Water-play was something that Bobby had still not tried out, much to my surprise. Children need water, and I always try to make sure that my playrooms have an easily accessible bathroom. (Oddly enough Bobby chose the day after Billy's Hour to play for the first time with the sprinkler in the bath.)

After the bath, Billy chose to sit on the toilet, and delight-edly did 'both' – or 'both' as far as he was concerned, since even if only wind emerged from one hole, plenty of the appropriate liquid emerged from the other. There is a natural stage, round about the age of two, when children want to urinate in the right place; they enjoy being in control of what comes out, when it comes out, and where to put it. Keeping them in nappies makes them start to feel that the process is dirty and nasty. Billy had quite clearly reached and passed this stage.

He had removed his nappy with his pants when he got undressed; I glanced at it where it lay on the floor, thinking no way was it going back on again. It didn't; it accompanied him home in a plastic bag. That was the beginning of Billy's toilet freedom – a happy landmark for him and something good for me to take to Los Angeles next day, although I had a heavy heart about leaving Bobby without formal Hours.

Los Angeles
I love Los Angeles. I remember on my first arrival there looking round at the tropical vegetation, and feeling I was in a fairyland. On this second visit the magic was still there, and my expectations were high. I met the head of the Counselling Clinic and most of its other staff, gave demonstrations and discussed my work with anyone interested, and was even offered the choice of a room in which I could eventually work.

While I was there I made a firm commitment to return to the clinic and start work there at the beginning of May. Looking at it now, the plan seems odd, but it seemed quite reasonable at the time. Robert Senior had told me that he might be moving to Los Angeles with his family, in which case the set-up would be ideal. In addition, I have never seen myself as the sort of person on whom a patient or child comes permanently to depend; I see myself as a starter, training people who can take over from me, so that my methods can be spread as widely as possible. I knew that I could if necessary replace myself with Bobby by getting in a trained worker from the Toronto clinic. If the worst came to the worst, L.A. to New York, although not quite commutable, is nonetheless a perfectly possible journey.

One of the children I gave Hours to during this visit was a little boy called Bruce. Bruce, like Bobby, was an outstandingly original child; he was about five, and his background appeared at surface glance to be exactly opposite to Bobby's. His parents were very likeable but suffered from problems of emotional immaturity, and Bruce was for all practical purposes a member of a group family: that is, a group of adults who agree to act as parents to all the children of the group. The children know that they have a *right* to the parental care of all the adults, this care extending to such things as meals, bed, listening to problems, etc., when their own parents are busy, in a bad mood, or simply not at that moment preferred. I have never seen this degree of attention totally attained, although I have been told of groups who claim to practise it successfully.

The contrast between Bruce and Bobby is of interest. They were both intelligent, independent children, well able to take care of themselves, at an age when the public could not accept that they were; their backgrounds were very different however, and I can't help wondering whether, if I had been in L.A. 'doing' Bruce instead of in New York 'doing' Bobby, I would have been able to get the police on my side, as I was to do with Bobby in New York and later in London.

It was while with Bruce in Los Angeles that I first became aware of an aspect of American life which was to become one of the major hazards of my undertakings with Bobby – 'compensation-claim phobia'. In our travels in America, and later in London, we were to come across a number of people who, finding an apparently lost Bobby, would be genuinely concerned and in his interest call the police. These people markedly contrasted with those whose concern for a child's safety was purely insurance-motivated.

Bruce and I were in a café one day. Bruce was kneeling on

his chair, holding on to the back of it and making small rocking movements so that the front legs came a little off the ground. He had been doing this with great intentness for quite a long time while I gave him full attention, and the distance that the front legs rose from the ground was gradually increasing. Bruce was in absolute control and knew exactly where the balance point was. Eventually, he tipped over his balance point and landed, unhurt, on the floor. The café owner leaped across the room and picked him up, ignoring my request to leave him alone and let him pick himself up. There was real panic in that man's eyes, and I could see quite clearly the cause of the panic – the possibility that if Bruce were hurt I would sue him for damages. After scolding Bruce and me and relieving his anxiety by finding no broken bones – his concern for Bruce being exactly nil – he said to me: 'If that kid had been hurt I might have had an action taken out against me!'

After he had gone, Bruce looked at me almost in tears and said, quietly and gently, 'I did it on purpose – I planned that fall – I knew I wouldn't hurt myself.'

While I was in Los Angeles, Robert Senior was also there on business and I saw him on several occasions. Once we sat in his car and had a long talk about Children's Hours, and once he took me out to dinner. The most valuable occasion was when I arranged for him to observe me giving an Hour to a child; the child was Bruce.

Robert not only observed me take an Hour with Bruce; he also gave an Hour to Bruce. This was the first time I had incorporated a parent in this way, and it was very successful.

The Hours took place in a ramshackle house (I think the roof fell in while I was there) with a rather ramshackle not-garden, with several cars in it which were being repaired by Bruce's father. The front door was always open, and the house furnished comfortably, but by no means smartly, with a general air of being a communal place; it was a warmly lived-in mess. Into this background the conventional Robert relaxed and sank happily; he observed well, without effort and without interference. He quite clearly liked Bruce, and Bruce was equally happy to have him as an observer.

When it was his turn to give Bruce an Hour he was so relaxed in himself, as he recapped all that the child did and said, that I felt he was fully identifying with Bruce. Somehow the child was giving the grown man something he lacked; both sessions were valuable to both people.

I had not yet seen him in relationship to Bobby, but I know that it would have been impossible for him to give Bobby this kind of unjudgemental observation. This is the usual case with parents, who feel that they must adopt a parental role with their children; playing the strong adult, pointing things out, educating, and, too often, criticizing.

5 Building a Team

Return to New York
I lost no time in returning from Los Angeles. I kept my last
appointment and boarded the first available plane. Once on
the plane I began to be aware of my anxieties about Bobby. I
had vivid memories of a boy in Canada; I had had to go to
England for two weeks very shortly after starting to give him
Hours; he became very disturbed and anxious, and until my
return retreated into over-eating as a cover for his distress.
My Bobby anxiety was increased when I got back and
learned that several of the voluntary helpers had failed to
show up. In all, he had been taken out only two or three
times during my absence.

The next day, when Bobby arrived for his Hour he instantaneously started to live and experience his freedom in
and around my flat. He spared not a second to greet me in
any way; he wasn't going to waste any learning time on such
trivia; for all he was able to know, this might be his last unit
of freedom, and he was not going to lose a jot of it.

Now that Bobby and I have been separated, four times in
all, I realize that on each occasion I have expected to find
that he has slipped back. I have been slow to learn just how
exceptional a child Bobby is; he just won't slip back. Any
forward progress he makes in life, skill or security will be tied
up, knotted and sealed. No treasure of experience is going to
slip through his fingers.

He started his play just where he had left off, in just the
same way, exploring every new corridor, set of steps and
corner that he could find, using the lift and pressing

different buttons endlessly. I needn't have felt anxious, or even angry with the people who hadn't shown up; the anxiety and anger faded quickly; I got on with the job of listening to Bobby in the activities of his choice.

All the same, I was determined to get help of a more consistent kind. It was becoming clear to me and to Bobby's parents that Bobby needed much more attention than I was able to provide in the conventional Hour, and we decided that I should find a child-minder at a child-minder's rate of pay, who would take Bobby out for much of the day, bringing him to me for his Hour during or after this time. So I set about finding such a person, someone who would be able to cooperate with my methods even if totally ignorant of child psychology.

It is part of the policy of Children's Hours not just to do it, but to teach it (and eventually write about it). The standard method of teaching is to have observers and recorders present at sessions, who ultimately learn to give Hours themselves. As this work was relatively unknown in New York, people were not lining up to learn about it; it soon became apparent that they would have to be hired, and I treated all hired assistants as students. As the scale of operations increased, the number of helpers we needed increased. The total agreed sum of money was exhausted long before the appointed date. I asked for more; Robert Senior did not have it to give; we struggled on without it.

Eileen had commitments of her own. I asked around my friends, acquaintances and fellow-tenants, and during that week at least half a dozen young people came to observe my Hours with Bobby and Billy. There was Andrew, a student of Japanese; he was to become a lifelong friend. There was Joe the actor, and Reg, a social worker whom I met at a co-counselling group in one of the flats. I was always very pleased to get men observers; males are at a premium in this work, and I noticed that Bobby seemed to have a real need for maleness. There were several others, male and female, and I hoped that I could find some students among them. Many of them however only came once, out of interest or curiosity, and vanished out of my life again.

In Canada we had a standard procedure for introducing observers and I tried to follow the same procedure with Bobby. First of all they would be given a brief set of instructions:

'Go in there and behave as a medical student in an operating theatre. Greet the child in an ordinary way when you are introduced, but do nothing else unless asked to by the child. Take off that smile which you have on your face! Whatever emotion is trapped in that smile, it is *your* emotion, and your emotion has no place in the playroom. Keep a straight face unless the child invites a response, in which case give the response that the child is inviting.'

That last instruction sounds tough, but it's very important. People want to be liked; they think that if they smile, the child will think they're nice. But the essence of therapy is to be serious, doubly so with children. In Toronto we were visited by a lot of Chinese doctors and it was really difficult teaching them how not to smile!

If the child becomes the centre of the observer's attention the observer will naturally reflect the child's emotions. If he is asked to participate by the child, he should do exactly what the child wants him to do. If the child does not wish to involve the observer then he must remain strictly an observer, with a straight face.

Participation might mean playing a part in the child's fantasy – a monster, for instance, a loving parent, or an enemy to be shot. I remember one sweet natured little girl in Canada who lined up a whole team of observers whom she verbally 'punished' with sadistic ferocity! Bobby was as yet a long way from using observers in this way, but he accepted their presence when I introduced them with a brief 'Hi Bobby, this is Andrew.' He didn't respond to this introduction, but he would have made it quite clear if he had wanted them removed. The child of course has the right to veto an observer if it chooses; Bobby, however, quickly realized that the observers were a part of my team, and never raised any objections. They were not as yet real people to him, but they were a part of me. And after their introduction they would follow us out into the lifts, up and down the stairs, and onto the roof – wherever Bobby chose to go.

Some of the observers felt as anxious as I had the first time they saw Bobby run to the balustrade and look over, but briefed by me they controlled their anxiety. I would explain to them that the person who gets carried away by panic emotions under such circumstances is actually creating the next accident by showing his fear to a child. This destroys the child's confidence in his ability to take care of himself. I have seen accidents caused in this way – for example when a child climbing perfectly safely on a roof, with his limbs and sense of balance in coordination, was grabbed at by an anxious adult – and fell.

Bobby never stayed long by the balustrade. He had discovered a particular private place that contained the most enchantment for him: his 'room', one of the storage sheds. It was a mess, it was a junkhole, but to Bobby it was special. The way the door opened was special, the way you walked into it was special, the way the dust and the cobwebs were there was special. I have lost count of the times that Bobby visited it. To me it was reminiscent of *The Secret Garden*.* It was Bobby's holy place.

It was Bobby's delight at going on the roof, together with some difficult encounters with the less tolerant tenants where I was staying, that made me realize how desperately Bobby needed space in which he could stretch his new-found wings. He was by now darting into every lift he could guess might be present behind an openable door. As I watched him bolt from one place to another, treating human beings as so many obstacles to be navigated, my mind travelled back

* Frances Hodgson Burnett (Heinemann, 1911)

to my own childhood, where a vast, sparsely inhabited countryside was the saviour of my sanity as I escaped into it from the adults indoors who so impeded my freedom. I thought, 'That's what I had, that's what I'll give to Bobby.' I thought around to where I knew space existed and where I knew enough people who would be willing to give me support. Provincetown on Cape Cod was the place. There Bobby and Billy too could have the freedom of the beach and sea.

I had first been to Provincetown while I was in Canada. I had gone there for a conference, and had been given a very warm welcome. I had a lot of good friends there, including Doug, who had been a member of our Toronto staff and was now a school-teacher, and Barbara Baker, who worked at the Provincetown Counselling Centre and with whom I had many philosophical ideas in common. So, as well as offering sea and space, Provincetown would enable me to operate from a secure base among people who understood my work. And I would be able to give much more time to the boys than the Hours they were getting in New York.

I consulted Robert and Louise who, after some consideration, agreed. Plans were made for us to set off on 12 April. Phone calls were made; a holiday apartment was booked, and my Provincetown friends offered to look out for suitable assistants – I could see that being with Bobby and Billy full-time would require a good deal of energy.

It was decided that Louise and the baby should come with us. Although the boys behaved as though they did not need their mother, and appeared to ignore her, they did need her presence, Bobby in particular. I did not want to remove him from his mother just at the stage when he was starting to emerge from his cocoon-like state. Our party would be completed by my new assistant, Mimi, whom I had just taken on.

Mimi was an ex-girlfriend of one of the young men who worked for the management at the place where I was staying. Knowing that I was looking for help, he had told me that she had worked in a family as an au pair; that he thought she was good with children, and that she was at a loose end. I set up an appointment to meet her that same afternoon.

When Mimi arrived at my apartment for the interview my first impression was of a tall, shy, soft-spoken girl with a ready smile and eagerness to please. I had forebodings about this eagerness; I had too often seen this quality as a protective covering for a character that cannot stand up to strong personalities. As a boss I am capable of being very domineering, and I need the people who work with me to be able to stand up to me. Would Mimi crumble? At that first interview I feared that she might. I nonetheless hired her to start work the following week. I have never regretted it.

Billy was due for his second Hour that week, so I plunged Mimi in at the deep end and had her observing and recording his Hour, followed by an Hour with Bobby.

Billy's Hours were going easily. He continued to enjoy his water-play and control of his urination, and I continued to send him home without a nappy. With Bobby, toilet-training was a different matter, and one of Mimi's tasks would be to help to get him out of his nappies.

For my first few sessions with Bobby I had ignored the nappies. I told him he was free in my room and bathroom to take his clothes off if he wished, but he did not. On one occasion Bobby was smelling with dirty nappies, and I told him that I could not take him in the lift if he smelt. We went down the stairs. He protested, but he came.

Just over a week after my return from Los Angeles his nappies were once again smelly when it was time to leave. Bobby started heading for the lift and I told him that if he wanted to go into it, I would take his nappies off. Bobby protested loudly; I believe that he hated those nappies as much as I did, and his bottom was always sore in those days; but to have them removed offended his dignity.

This time, I insisted. Screaming, Bobby persisted in his 'Nos' while I took his trousers down, wiped his bottom and replaced his trousers. (How I grew to hate those trousers, and longed for plain, easy elastic tops or shoulder bibs, designed for easy changing and comfort for the child!) It was one of those awful occasions when an adult gets his way by force in the teeth of a protesting child. I apologized to him continually throughout: 'I'm sorry Bobby, if we go in the lift with shit pants the other people won't like it, I'm very sorry Bobby.' One should always apologize to a child when doing by force something it doesn't want done. Afterwards I felt awful. I felt awful at having engaged in a power struggle with a child, something I always try to avoid, although having made that initial mistake I had to carry the struggle through to the end and win it.

The next day, however, Bobby had a breakthrough! I would never get involved deliberately in a rage-producing situation, and on the rare occasions when it happens I die seven deaths with remorse, but almost without exception the child breaks through the next day. I do not understand how this happens; it happened on this occasion.

When people ask me how I know there has been a break-through, I find it very hard to answer. As I do not look at an unwell person as a set of symptoms, I do not look at a well or growing person as a set of absent symptoms. I tune in to the whole person and know that a change has taken place.

When I met Bobby the next day, he had changed, he was a step nearer maturity. When it was time to go, he had once again shit his pants. This time he made the choice; he simply said, 'Down the stairs.' And down the stairs we went, with no trouble.

Bobby spent a large part of his next Hour with me playing with the Life game, turning the wheel and counting the numbers. At one point there was a long silence lasting perhaps three minutes, while he just sat there and looked and looked. There was an observer present, the social worker called Reg, who was sitting behind: I could see Reg wishing he could watch Bobby's face. It was a fabulous silence. I couldn't see the clock, since all my attention was on Bobby, but I was thinking, 'I wish I could time this silence.' I couldn't help wondering if Bobby was telepathic, because when it was over he went straight to the clock.

He manoeuvred the clock and said, 'Hour over at twelve.' I was beginning to understand his speech by now. I said, 'No, because Hour's over at ten' – meaning when the big hand was at ten to the hour. He repeated, 'Because Hour's over at ten.' This was the first small child with whom I had been who found the fifty-minute Hour to be a problem. Bobby understood the concept of an hour, and I was giving him fifty minutes. His puzzlement was one of the many signs of his unusual quality.

Then Bobby went round my room, checking out the things he knew to be dangerous. I always gently said 'Dangerous!' as he approached them. Reg commented afterwards that he seemed to have to go back to those things again and again, the cooker, the heater and so on, as if 'he was going into battle to conquer something'. Of course, he was.

After that we went up on the roof, where it was raining, and into 'Bobby's room'. He was in a very thoughtful mood, and took little notice of Reg, which was unusual with a male observer.

Looking back, I can see Bobby's breakthrough continuing during the whole of this Hour. His reluctance to come upstairs, instead of immediately rushing into my flat, the silence, the taking time to understand, the thoughtful air, all this was new. It indicated a wider awareness of himself and of me, and a new freedom from the compulsion to engage in constant, frenzied activity. This continued when the Hour was over. We had one of our best goodbyes ever. When he had to be removed forcibly, kicking and screaming and trying to hang on to doors and walls, I always felt like a murderer. This time, when I said 'It's time to leave,' he started his usual delaying tactics, saying, ''nother minute! 'nother minute!' I said, 'OK,' and gave him another minute.

Then I said, 'Well, you've had your minute, Bobby, shall I take you by the hand or will you come?' And I didn't have to take him by the hand; he took mine willingly and started to go down the stairs.

Then he stopped and came up again, saying, 'No. Lift.' I said, 'Yes, that's OK, the lift, no shit pants today.' It was one of the times when I appeared to break my own rules by interpreting; in fact, I was recapping what I knew that he was thinking.

Reg and I had a talk about this Hour afterwards. Since he was a qualified social worker with a concern for kids, I was interested in what he thought of it. Among his comments, he said: 'I was struck by Bobby's insatiable appetite for testing everything, to see how it works and to relate it to what he already knows. I was struck that he also felt at home everywhere he went. Everything there was for him to try out. He felt very "allowed" to look at things . . .

'I thought it was really exciting. It seemed there was so much happening with so much energy that he has, that you're allowing him to get out. This sort of letting him take control and following him, it's really exactly what he needs, and the little I know about children it seems it's what all children need.'

The next day was 3 April; Bobby had been with me for exactly a month. That evening I drew up a kind of informal assessment of Bobby's progress. Here are some extracts from it:

D.D.I.: At first Bobby only understood one thing, which was that the adult would prohibit him from doing anything, whatever he wanted to do, so he rushed madly in and did it. Bobby now understands when I say 'dangerous' in the tone of voice of 'Be careful,' or when I say, 'I don't want that broken' in the tone of voice of 'I don't want that broken,' or what the other chaps in the lift won't like. He understands the difference between danger, damage and impropriety and accepts my prohibitions for what they are.

I have no difficulty in enforcing limits with Bobby at all now. It's a little difficult with things like my tape recorder when he says, 'Bobby do it,' because he wants to do it so quickly that he puts the tape in wrong; but that will only be short-lived.

INTELLIGENCE: Bobby's intelligence is phenomenal. I do not want to do an ordinary IQ test, but the example I will give here is that he pressed the lift button for 'PH' which didn't work. He tried it once or twice, and then later, when he was up on the roof in one of the derelict rooms, he suddenly paused and thought for a bit and said, 'This is PH.' His intelligence in my opinion is connected with his problem.

PEE AND SHIT: We have not yet tackled the nappy problem. There was one occasion when I changed him forcibly and there was the occasion when he peed on the linoleum by the lift and I went and fetched a floor cloth. Before it arrived he was spreading it all around the floor, and I dealt with that in quite an ordinary way. Plans are now being made starting on Monday: Mimi, who is a new member of our staff, is going to take and babysit him from nine till twelve every morning, after which she is going to bring him here for an Hour. She in her own way is going to try to get those nappies off.

DICTION: Bobby's diction is still difficult to understand but it has improved. He does say whole sentences now and some of his sentences are understandable.

EMOTION: On one or two occasions he has smiled at me. He has shown overt affection to two of my helpers. He relates to nearly all observers. Yesterday there was a man observer whom he hardly related to at all, which is unusual.

PLAY MATERIAL: For the first part of the month Bobby played with the lift all the time, going up and down and pressing the buttons and getting out and running around and trying to ring doorbells, which he now doesn't do unless he's frustrated. Then he found the roof and he played with the roof a lot, going up and looking over the edge, going into the disused room, up at the side, and for the last three or four times he has been playing in my room, and doing water-play, and wheel-play on one of the games, where he plays a sort of roulette. At all times he has played with the clock. He is obsessed with numbers.

OVERALL PROGRESS: I am very well satisfied with the way he is going.

In fact, Bobby was already a changed child. It was gorgeous. In my diary I wrote: 'He will not be institutionalized now. He will grow up into an extremely worthwhile, able person and the time and the energy spent now will be very much worth it.'

A week later, just before we left for Provincetown, I had another power-struggle and breakthrough episode with Bobby. He was 'playing me up' by turning the handles of all the flat doors that he wasn't supposed to knock on, and I was saying, 'I'm sorry, we won't knock on that door,' and pulling him away from them. I pulled him away from one door rather violently, which I should not have done in an Hour. Bobby cried. I watched him sitting there, rubbing the tears away from his eyes with his two hands, as much as to say, 'I'm not allowed to cry and I'm not going to cry.' Then the Hour proceeded as usual, although I felt awful.

The next day, he gave me his first actual demonstration of affection. He had set up a kind of game which I won; he came over and touched my cheek with his cheek. During the Hour he smiled a lot, glowing with happiness and affection, and towards the end he had his pants off and was running around with a naked bottom. In fact, he went right down to the foyer with a naked bottom, and I had to retrieve him, thinking privately that it was a very good thing I had done so much PR work with the reception staff and other tenants. If that had been his first Hour, it would probably have been the last! It was a bit of a dilemma but only a small one; pants off in public was not good PR, but for Bobby to run around with pants off was a triumph!

Mimi was present on that occasion; she had been working with us for just a week, and tells her own story in the next chapter.

6 *Mimi* (by Mimi)

I had had a succession of jobs when Rachel hired me as companion to Bobby after she had heard about me from my ex-boyfriend. She called me one morning when I had come in from a mile run in Central Park, and asked when we could meet. It was a Saturday, and I suggested Monday evening. She said, 'How about now?' So we made a date for later that afternoon at her flat. That was my first taste of one big difference in our attitudes to life: Mimi says there's plenty of time; Rachel says there's no time to lose.

I dressed neatly but casually, as it was a job interview for a kid job, and went across town to Rachel's apartment block, a big old building on upper Broadway. I stated my destination at the lobby desk, was waved through, and took a creaky lift to the fifth floor. I knocked on Rachel's apartment door and a gravelly English voice told me to come in. The door was unlocked, unusual in New York, so I walked in and got a glimpse of a desk and a bed before Rachel moved into my field of vision from the adjoining bathroom. She was an oldish woman, grey-haired, compactly built, wearing a simple knit shirt and trousers. She walked with a slight limp, but the impression I got of her was of strength rather than frailty.

I was hesitating about how to address her, 'Doctor'? 'Miss Pinney'? when she said, 'Call me Rachel. And you must be Mimi.'

Her manner cut through my polite 'job interview front' as she presented me with the problem of the two kids, Bobby and Billy. Billy was due to arrive soon, and she briefed me on how to behave as an observer-recorder of an Hour, so that I could see her method at work before making any decisions. Then she went downstairs to meet him and I looked around her room. It was very neat, furnished starkly with used furniture. There were two beds, one serving as a sofa, and two desks pushed together as an office nook. A compact refrigerator and a two-burner hot plate made up the kitchen. Along one wall were boxes and shelves of play material, her stock-in-trade for Children's Hours. A large window over her bed looked across a dim courtyard.

Rachel came back into the room with Billy, an insubstantial-looking little boy with rather transparent skin. He seemed anxious, as if waiting for a restraining hand or a voice telling him 'No'; at the same time he smiled, though not with his eyes, at me. He seemed to need some encouragement from Rachel to let loose for his Hour, but then went quickly from thing to thing, running around, strewing toys, playing in Rachel's bath, and running out of the door. Rachel followed him paraphrasing his words and 'listening' to his behaviour, and I followed them, watching and scribbling madly.

Billy didn't seem like a terribly disturbed kid; more like an ordinary 'naughty' boy, doing the forbidden in order to make the grown-up notice. Rachel had explained to me that the essence of her therapy was that the 'taker' takes full notice of everything done or said; the only things forbidden were real danger, real damage, and real impropriety. The grown-ups kept those real limits, but otherwise the kid was free; there was no direction given or judgements made. The theory made sense; it was like other non-judgemental therapies I had met.

However, I was used to grown-ups in therapy, who sat and talked quietly; Billy racing around and making messes, with Rachel paraphrasing his jabbering, seemed chaotic to me. But I saw too that she was in control. When Billy wanted to play with a bin of flour, Rachel put gentle but firm limits on how much he could use: 'I think we'll be very careful with that flour, Billy. It's food, and I don't want food to be wasted, so you can use just a little of the flour. That's it, Billy. Thank you. And now you're mixing it with some water. You say you're making supper, are you? I see, you're making supper.'

At one point he was interested in Rachel's cassette tape recorder and she became directive enough to explain how it functioned, so that he wouldn't accidentally break it. 'I think we'll press just one button at a time, lad. That's it. Thank you, lad.' Rachel's tone was not sharp; she neither scolded nor set up a struggle for power. She was with him in his exploration while still keeping him from damaging the tape recorder.

When Billy's Hour was over, Rachel thought it would be good for me to meet Bobby too, so she rang his mother to ask if she'd bring him over. Louise came straight away; when they arrived, Rachel went to meet Bobby in the lobby, and brought him back with her.

Though looking enough like Billy to make it easy at first to confuse them, at second look I could see Bobby was altogether different. His body was more substantial, his hair a little darker and thicker; and then, his face was his own: mouth pursed, even grim, and unreadable dark brown eyes. He would not look directly at me, barely took notice of me. I felt that the real person was somewhere deep inside.

Bobby went directly to Rachel's digital alarm clock, and mumbled numbers to himself while he turned the dial. Then he wanted to leave the room and took Rachel's hand to open the door. This was classic autistic behaviour, Rachel told me later. We went down the hallway towards the lifts, me taking notes behind them. Passing the two regular lifts, Bobby stopped at the one used by the maintenance people and indicated by pointing and grunts that he wanted to be picked up. Rachel said she wasn't able to pick him up because of her lame leg, but if it was okay with both of us, I could. So I touched Bobby for the first time, holding him up to see through the little window into the lift shaft. He was hard to hold as he pressed against the window, then reached over to press the call button, then shifted back to the window.

I felt I was a step-stool to him. There was no communication, no expectation that I would join in his delight at button-pushing or lift-waiting. The lift did not arrive; it was operable only by key, we discovered later, so when Bobby had had enough, he went on down the hall.

When the Hour was over, Rachel had me escort Bobby downstairs to meet Louise in the lobby. Bobby went with me easily enough, but the moment he caught sight of his mother he threw himself down on the floor screaming, then hid behind me, and then tried to go back upstairs. I felt at a loss, but was not as embarrassed as Louise, who seemed to be torn between stepping forward to claim her boy and blending into the background. Somehow I got the two of them together and retreated back to Rachel's.

I wasn't sure what I had just been part of, or whether it was a good idea to get further involved, but there was something compelling about those kids. They were real people; salvageable children, with a real need that I could choose to meet. And Rachel was clearly a person of integrity, offering to employ me and train me to do something that mattered. If it was unconventional, so much the better. And on the practical side, the pay and hours would be good, with no special dress needed! So, we agreed to work together.

On Monday 4 April I started work properly. I was to be with Bobby from three to five hours a day, five days a week. I was not, and was not expected to be, a trained therapist; Rachel's term for me was 'enlightened babysitter', and my times with him were called 'Special Times', as distinguished from her 'Hours'.* My task was to be with him, and as far as possible let him do what he wanted to do; giving him the run of the town that he wanted so badly.

Each day in that week I met Bobby and his father by the

* In time these two terms became synonymous

front door of my building, a ten-minute walk from their place. They'd ring the doorbell, I'd buzz them in and then go the four flights downstairs. Robert Senior would hand over a change of trousers and underpants in case Bobby soiled what he was wearing, and then went off to his office.

Bobby did not want to share my attention, and after the first couple of days would say 'Bye-bye, Daddy' upon coming through the door. Then he would take his time getting to know my stairway, savouring the process of the climb, mumbling the floor-numbers on the wall and the numbers of the apartments we passed. I was used to running up the stairs two at a time, so it seemed to take forever with Bobby, until I realized that there was no real need to hurry. I was with him, not he with me.

Then we would usually spend an hour or so in my apartment while Bobby checked out all the machinery in the place. An early favourite was my sewing machine, whose drive belt resembled the moving steps of an escalator! Bobby spoke a little bit, parroting television game-show hosts, yelling or mumbling to himself, 'You win!' and 'Cash and prizes!' But he would not respond to hearing his name spoken, or to any direct requests, nor would he speak directly to me.

The first day we were together I decided we would set off across Central Park, and picnic on the way, before meeting Rachel at her place for his daily Hour. It was my first realization that my idea of a good time might be totally alien to Bobby. He didn't like the sandwiches I'd made, or sitting on a rock to eat them; and he got tired before we reached our destination. When I tried to carry him piggy-back to speed our progress, he screamed in fear of falling, and wanted me to carry him with my arms around him. I bullied my way through, shouting to his screaming, sometimes carrying him, sometimes leading him by the hand, which he tried to avoid my taking.

When we emerged on Rachel's side of the Park he saw

taxis and buses and ran towards them, clearly wanting to ride. To my grown-up mind, the distance to be covered wasn't worth the expense of a cab, and the bus wasn't going the right way, so we didn't take either but slowly fought our way to Rachel's. When we got to her door Bobby immediately forgot about me and went in. I retreated quickly, grateful to have an hour free of him.

I was upset and disillusioned. I had always thought of myself as a patient person who was good with kids, and I had always thought that kids enjoyed parks, picnics and piggyback rides. I saw to my shame that with Bobby I had changed into a raving maniac, and resolved to keep my temper when I took him to his home.

The plan was for me to fetch him after his Hour, simply drop him off at his apartment, then return alone to Rachel's to talk over the day. Simply dropping him off turned out to be about as easy as simply crossing the Park had been earlier in the day. He didn't want to go home; all the attractions of doorways, shops and escalators were gone after in a frenzy, as he stalled for more time outside. I didn't know whether to give in to him a little or a lot or not at all. I didn't know how impatiently they awaited him at home or Rachel awaited me across town. But I wanted my day with him to be over, so I prevented a lot of that exploration with constant talk, occasional hand-holding and much apologizing, as instructed by Rachel: 'Sorry, Bobby, your time is up. We won't go into Woolworth's, I'm sorry we're going home now. We're not riding that lift today. Not today, sorry, I think we won't go in that building. We're going home.'

Once inside his home building the going got easier, though in the lift he pressed most of the buttons between the lobby and our destination. Finally the doors opened on a quiet carpeted hallway and he led the way to his apartment. He pointed to the doorbell and I lifted him up to ring it.

There was a small struggle when the door opened, as Billy tried to get out and Bobby tried not to go in, but between

Louise and me, everyone was wrestled in, and the door shut
and bolted. The boys raced off together into another room,
and I talked a little bit with Louise and Doreen, the large
Jamaican woman who helped her with cleaning and kid-
minding. Louise and her home were carefully kept. She was
dressed in a sweater and trousers, her dark hair in a perfect
page-boy, her face carefully made up. Bobby had her dark
brown eyes.

The apartment had large windows hung with plants, and
was decorated with modern furniture, framed prints, and
objets d'art. It did not feel like a place where two active boys
and a baby lived. I went in to the boys' room to say goodbye, noticing as I went latches high up on all the doors. The
window in their room was covered with a heavy steel mesh;
Louise explained that they used to climb up against the
window and everyone was afraid they'd fall out so this safety
covering, which also blocked a lot of light, was installed. I
took my leave and went back to the foyer, thereby initiating
a scene of struggling and screaming as the boys tried to get
out of the open door after me and Louise and Doreen kept
them in.

At last the door closed and, alone in the corridor, I heaved
a sigh and went to the lift. I was too overwhelmed to make
any judgements but was glad I could leave that tempestuous
household until tomorrow.

Every day that first week I returned to Rachel's to discuss
the day's events with her and get her encouragement and
criticisms. Rachel was very patient with me and my temper,
but was always on the side of the kid. She had developed the
therapy, and, through conviction and long practice, could
totally switch off her own wants and needs when giving an
Hour. She knew that complete focusing of attention couldn't
be sustained for hours on end, but she urged me to give as
much as I could.

New to Rachel's methods, I was quite self-conscious without being self-aware. I would lose my temper before I

realized my patience was wearing thin, and then I would think the kid had pushed me over the edge.

I had a hard time too, sometimes, with the general public, not being a charming, grey-haired English doctor. Many people assumed I was Bobby's mother, and thought I was being negligent in letting him loose in public without a restraining hand; I didn't have the confidence to deliver a quick synopsis of the therapy to explain myself and educate them, as Rachel did. At times I let people get under my skin and would grab Bobby to try and make him behave more 'normally'. But most often I took refuge in the anonymity that New York is famous for, and let unsolicited comments roll off me, my attention and empathy being with Bobby. I relied a lot on Rachel to remind me that the job we were doing was right for the kid, that public opinion was not our barometer.

Bobby's need to explore things began eventually to touch something in me. I remembered my own childhood fascination with lifts, for instance. We gradually grew to be very fond of each other. I still smile when I think of the first positive communication we had. He and I were walking on the street, a little aimlessly, in no hurry. I got a sudden inspiration to speak to him in his own language. 'Ladies and gentlemen, I'd like to introduce you to the star of the show, and here he is, Bobby! Come on up here, Bobby, and say a few words to the studio audience.' He perked up at my 'game show' voice, looked closely, listened to the sweet sound, then grinned! The first time! A moment like that could carry me through a lot of frustrating times, showing me there was a real person inside the compulsive lift rider.

Rachel had hoped that I would be something of a secretary, keeping lists and diaries. The most I could do was to write daily reports of what Bobby and I did; she was on her own for the rest; paperwork is neither my skill nor my hobby. I don't know if she ever was reconciled to that. Like our opposite sleep rhythms: I am awake at night and she in the morning, and I believe that in her heart of hearts she thinks my morning fuzzy-headedness is due to some lack of moral fibre. The same applies to paperwork. Alongside these differences, however, there grew and still exists an appreciation of each other's strengths and talents which has carried us through, enabling us to cooperate with each other in getting the job done.

Many members of the public were critical, but I was armed against this by Rachel's counsel. We were acting in an unorthodox manner and we knew it. Most kids who were in therapy were indoors, not leading their therapists all over New York. Our method had its hazards, but weighed against the alternatives for Bobby, it was worth it. Without treatment his prognosis was institutionalization; we were trying to give him a future.

The trip to Provincetown (by Mimi)
I was used to the sort of journey where I get quietly on the train at one end, sit quietly in my seat reading a paperback or looking out at the passing scenery, and get quietly out at my destination.

The journey to Provincetown with Rachel, Bobby and Billy was not like that at all. Rachel refers to it as the real launch of our little team in public. I remember it as a trying, exhausting and embarrassing experience.

Louise and baby Abigail travelled from New York to Boston by plane; meanwhile Robert Senior took the rest of us by taxi to Grand Central Station, Rachel and I on guard to keep Billy from opening the doors, with Robert opposite us telling Billy to 'be a good boy'. When we got to the station Robert paid off the taxi and went on to work. Bobby immediately shot off into the crowd before Rachel could take his hand, diving and darting between legs, and was down on the platform way ahead of us. When we caught up with him Rachel was given a severe ticking off by the conductor for not looking after him properly.

We stowed our bags and sat down in our seats for a full half minute. Before the train had left the station, Bobby and Billy had got up to explore, each in a different direction, each followed by one of us. For the rest of that journey we walked (Rachel says we sprinted) up and down that train, almost non-stop, pressing the push-buttons which opened the doors between cars. Bobby loved that, of course; in and out of cars, up to one end of the train and back to the other. Sometimes there was a respite when we stood between the cars, looking out of the window, Bobby momentarily mesmerized and apparently soothed by the scenery rushing by. At one point, still not used to his new freedom from nappies, he dirtied his pants. As I cleaned him up in the tiny, lurching closet, I muttered and cursed and tried not to be judgemental about it. Bobby, however, wasn't upset by my reaction, in fact he seemed rather amused at it. Then we were back into motion again, up and down the corridors.

Of course we attracted attention; passengers and conductors looked at us with curiosity and sometimes annoyance. What sort of family was this, in which not only were the kids not made to sit in their seats but the mother and even the grandmother ran up and down the train with them? Rachel, catching someone's horrified glance as she raced by after Billy, would throw at them: 'These kids have never had any freedom – talk when I come back!' Dashing by a little later in the opposite direction, she would add, 'I'm a doctor from England and I'm helping these boys!' And on the third run past she would inform them: 'They've missed part of their childhood and I'm giving it back to them!'

Despite her limp and her grey hair, her stamina was amazing. I was wondering how much longer would it, could it, go on? But Rachel, completely tuned in to the boys and their needs, was enjoying their enjoyment and seemed tireless. Occasionally when our paths crossed she would PR me to keep up my flagging spirits! Though I don't consider myself a conformist, I was keenly conscious of the spectacle we created and had to keep pulling my attention away from myself to give it to Bobby and Billy. As yet I was far from being Rachel's colleague: I was her fumbling new assistant, needing every bit of the encouragement she gave me.

By the end of that four-and-a-half-hour journey, Rachel had somehow won over an entire trainload of passengers and most of the conductors. One woman borrowed her copy of *Dibs* and read it right through on the trip, and a young man called Peter temporarily joined the team. He was fascinated by what we were doing and wanted to know all about us. He lifted the boys to look through a window at the guards' van and gained our trust enough to take over with one of the pair while Rachel or I had a brief sit down.

Even the conductors eventually gave up trying to make us behave like normal passengers. After being PR'd at length by Rachel they would shrug their shoulders and say, 'Well . . . you're in charge.' One by one, she got them all on our side. Except, that is, for the conductor at the door of the first-class compartment at the end of one coach. In him Rachel and Bobby met their match. He stood solidly at the door; Bobby tried his usual ploy of ducking under an arm, but without success. Rachel said to Bobby: 'I'm afraid we can't go in there – the people in there are special people.'

Bobby's expression said 'Special people?'

Feeling she had not given Bobby sufficient explanation, Rachel turned to the conductor and said, 'What have those people got that we haven't, that they've spent so much money on?'

The conductor said simply: 'Me!' And Bobby never did get into that first-class compartment.

Finally we pulled in at Boston. Rachel and I carried the bags and kept a hand or an eye on each boy as we made our way through the station; not a direct journey, as Billy found an enormous baggage cart and, with the permission of its porter-owner, pushed it right across Boston Station. And back.

It was a wet day so Boston, a favourite city of mine, was obscured behind the rain-dripping windows of our taxi. No matter, as my attention had to be on the interior of the cab, repeating to Billy that I was sorry, he wasn't to open the car doors while we were moving.

At the airport we happily met up with Louise, tired after her own journey with a three-month-old baby, and got tickets for the flight to Provincetown. There was a short wait during which I followed Bobby as he discovered nearby escalators, lifts, lavatories and vending machines. Then the time came to board the plane, a lovely little twelve-seater. Rachel was delighted with it; she commented that it was a proper aeroplane, 'like we had in the old days'.

Bobby took one look at the instrument panel and tried to take the seat next to the pilot. Rachel took one look at the instrument panel and said firmly, 'I'm sorry, Bobby. Billy will sit in the front.' Bobby's response was to produce his habitual screech of frustration and to try to pull Billy out of the desired seat. Rachel explained, over and over again, 'I'm sorry, Bobby, the pilot is driving this plane and we must do what's right for him, I'm sorry, Bobby, you must sit with Mimi.' The pilot said nothing through all this, but looked grateful.

Rachel's methods sometimes look as though she doesn't take danger into account; this was an example of the many times she saw potential danger and took preventive action in advance. In fact, taking preventive action is an important feature of her method, rather than letting a child embark on a potentially dangerous course and stopping it half-way through, as so often happens in ordinary life.

So Billy, who so often had to take the back seat in our dealing with the two boys, happily sat in the place of honour, while Louise and the baby got settled and the other passengers joined us in the plane. Bobby protested about his seat the whole time we were in the air, not hysterically but doggedly, constantly fidgeting and repeating, 'Billy come back! Bobby sit up front!' And I kept up a stream of talk to let him know we wouldn't change our decision but that we knew about and sympathized with his feelings.

As we crossed Cape Cod Bay, the sky had cleared a little and some of the passengers, including Rachel, saw a whale spouting. Rachel was far more excited about the whale than the boys were; Bobby had no interest in what was going on outside, and I was giving him all my attention, intent on keeping him talking rather than screaming, so I missed the whale, though I saw some small islands and boats amid the choppy waters; the plane was almost disconcertingly low-flying.

Then we were over Provincetown, a tidy village on the inside of the sandy tip of Cape Cod, where the *Mayflower* pilgrims first set foot on American soil. Beyond the village we could see stretches of woods and sand-dunes, and beyond that the grey Atlantic. At last we landed, our journey over and further adventures about to begin.

We crossed the tarmac, preventing Bobby from boarding other small planes parked there, and entered the tiny terminal where we were met by Doug, Rachel's ex-colleague from Toronto. He was in his twenties, tall and boyishly handsome with dark curly hair, and dressed in bright water-proofs against the blustery April weather. He organized us into two relays and drove us to the apartment he had found for us. It was on the beach at the end of a wharf, the ground floor of a wooden, two-storied building, weathered but snug. It had two bedrooms, a sea-windowed sitting room with a balcony along two sides, a large kitchen and dining area and two bathrooms. It was furnished simply in nondescript motel style, and the television had already been removed at Rachel's request; we hadn't come this far to have the boys sit in front of a TV all day. We were all here to live and grow!

Rachel, used to England, marvelled over the luxury of 'things' provided by the landlord: saucepans, sheets, soap, toilet paper, etc. What was more, Doug had stocked up the kitchen and had a hot meal ready for us. As Rachel said, that was real friendship and hospitality; exactly what was needed at the right moment. Doug explained to Rachel that he was not going to be involved in the project himself, but would be a frequent visitor. And that's what he was, coming to us as a friend, Hour-giver and tour-guide, while keeping out of our administrative hassles.

After supper we looked at the bedroom situation and decided the boys should have the room with the twin beds, while Louise and the baby could take the other bedroom with the double bed and a cot. Rachel and I claimed the two day-beds in the sitting room. One or two small conflicts immediately arose. Louise had put on the central heating to keep the baby warm; Rachel went around opening all the windows to let in the fresh air. My problems began when I set about making the boys' beds. We had brought yards of heavy-gauge plastic to protect the mattresses from our two bed-wetters; Rachel wanted all the beds to be covered including mine, at which I balked. I could see no reason for it. I didn't want to sleep on crackling plastic, and I didn't wet my bed! It remained unplasticked.

That first night, and for the next few nights, we put the boys to bed at separate times. The idea was to treat them as two individual people, not as 'the boys', and also to 'divide and conquer': if one was already asleep the other was more likely to go to sleep. So I took long walks with Bobby on the first two nights while Billy was bedded, then 'did' Bobby when we got back.

Rachel also asked Louise to go out with the baby while the boys were put to bed; this was in order to avoid anything like their New York pattern of playing Momma up at bedtime. Louise complied, and once Bobby was asleep I ran out with a large note to tape on to the wharf where she would see it, 'Coast is clear. Welcome home Louise.' Eventually she came in, and told me she had seen Bobby and me walking outside but stood in some shadows so she wouldn't intrude on our quiet twosome. She was playing her role by ear, very anxious to do the right thing and not sure what that was.

Bobby explores Provincetown (by Rachel)
The next day started well. I had slept off my exhaustion of the day before and was up bright and early; so was Billy. Leaving the rest of the party still sleeping, Billy and I went out onto the beach. We travelled along the water's edge in a typical child fashion, squeezing under the supporting posts of outjutting balconies. We were happy; we were relaxed; we were children. I was not implementing any particular method; I was just being my natural self out with a child.

It was chilly but not cold, getting warmer as the sun rose higher over the horizon, and Billy asked if he could go into the sea. On receiving my 'Of course', he went straight into the water up to his knees, splashing happily; when he came out I took off his wet shoes and trousers and carried them. He arrived home with his top clothed and his bottom naked. We were both still happy.

When Louise saw us she was perturbed – she told me later that she was perturbed because he looked cold; I did her less than credit by assuming that she minded his being half-naked and that he had got his shoes, which turned out to be Bobby's shoes, wet. Louise, I felt, would have the children warm, looking nice and clean; I would have them free even if cold, looking anyhow and dirty.

Both Billy and I had enjoyed our early-morning outing, and in my naivety I expected to enjoy vast quantities of similar, ordinary seaside outings. For ordinary child-and-grown-up activities, buckets and spades are essential, so immediately after breakfast I went out to get some.

As it was off season, buckets and spades were not easy to find, but at last one obliging store-keeper searched his basement and found some. I returned triumphantly to the apartment with my trophies, to find Mimi, whom I'd left with Louise and the boys, tearing her hair out. She could cope with Bobby on his own but the two boys together made more screaming chaos than she knew how to handle.

Mimi was relieved to leave Louise in peace with Abigail and come out with me on the beach to demonstrate to the boys what to do with buckets and spades. We grown-ups enjoyed the simple play of digging holes and making castles, but the boys' lack of interest in conventional beach-play could not have been more absolute. Billy squashed flat anything we built, and Bobby screamed at the gritty feel of sand on his hands. In no time at all he was away, with me after him, bent on exploration.

Before my older legs could catch up with him he shot down the basement steps of a nearby house, found the front door open, ducked under the arm of the householder and went quickly round the house, looking for buttons to press. When I arrived I beamed my thanks for the hospitality before the woman had the chance to throw us both out, removed Bobby and made a mental resolution to return the next day to apologise and explain.

From that first morning, Bobby treated this out-of-season holiday resort as a poor edition of New York. He 'did' Provincetown as thoroughly as a tourist 'does' a foreign town. Tourists, however, usually have guidebooks and pay one visit to the places which someone else has chosen. Bobby was his own guidebook and places of his selection were visited many, many times.

Within hours of that first morning in Provincetown it was known that we were there. Bobby was so strikingly different that he couldn't pass unnoticed. To begin with, there was the extraordinary speed with which he moved. Although his movements still looked mechanical, they were not awkward; he seemed to glide swiftly from place to place without apparently moving his arms or legs. He moved so fast that he gave the impression of having transferred himself from point A to point B without any intervening movement. You and I walk or run; Bobby just got there.

In addition, any strangers who might be around at the time were treated simply as objects, like trees. He never looked at them directly, but wore a fixed, glassy stare, intent on what he was doing. To some of the people who saw him for the first time the overall effect was frightening. He flew past, in and out of people's legs, under their arms, like a sleepwalker or a ghost, not acknowledging their existence or communicating with them in any way. People know how to react to a cat, a dog, even a wild animal escaped from the zoo, but they didn't know how to respond to this fast-moving animal because they got no response from him.

The population of Provincetown includes a community of Portuguese fishermen, and a number of big-city refugees, including artists, painters and writers. A number of them are themselves unorthodox, and are on the whole more ready to accept unorthodox behaviour in others. The less accepting ones, like those in New York, did not believe that Bobby would do no damage, neither did they believe that he was safe, so we had lots of copies made of the following card, to be handed out as and when necessary:

Children's Hours
To any neighbour or observer who may be interested in, critical of or annoyed by our kids:

We believe that kids *need* units of complete attention from one adult. These units are called 'Johnnie Hours' or 'Mary Hours'. Kids with problems get better and every kid grows after receiving these hours.

Please bear with us if some of the things you see look odd. Dr. Pinney will be very happy to explain further. (Address given)

A number of people did accept Bobby for what he was, and those who did were accepted by him. These included the many friends I already had in Provincetown, who started visiting us from the moment we arrived, and Katie, the wife of the manager of the apartment house where we were staying, and who was acting as manager in his absence. There was also a nice family who were renting the apartment above ours; there were three children, and the mother was a teacher. The moment she spotted Bobby she said, 'That kid is an autistic, isn't he?'

I said, 'Yes, but we don't say that word out loud.' I would cheerfully explain Bobby and what we were doing within his hearing, but I was rigid about that label not being used.

This family had a telescope set up on their balcony, which could be reached by steps from our apartment. It was an obvious Bobby-attraction, and the father would have let him play with it, but a telescope is a telescope and fine adjustments have a way of going wrong in unskilled hands, so we immediately undertook to ensure that Bobby did not go up the steps unescorted. We were friends with the family throughout their stay; on the Sunday of our first week the thirteen-year-old son Peter observed Billy having an Hour, at his own request.

Once all these people had been seen by Bobby to be part of my entourage he accepted them and to some extent acknowledged their existence, as he had done with the helpers and observers who had joined us in New York.

It was very early on during this trip, probably on the train, that Mimi and I realized that now we were embarking on a twenty-four hour programme we would have to break with strict Children's Hours rules, as Mimi had already been doing in New York. It is simply not possible to be fully attentive, non-directive and non-evaluative for twenty-four hours a day, even if working in shifts, which we did once we were joined by assistants. So it was decided that like Mimi, any helpers we hired should give the boys Special Times which would be open-ended and also not quite as free as an Hour. I took Special Times too, and Doug and I gave both the boys formal Hours as well.

During that first day I realized that another arrangement would have to be reconsidered: the question of Louise.

Taking Mum with us was certainly the right thing to do. Bobby was only four, and he was a disturbed four, who had cut himself off from human relationships at the age of approximately nine months. No child of nine months can exist without a mother figure of some sort; Bobby needed his mother and I could not replace her. In addition he had some powerful double emotions towards Louise, and he made full use of the Provincetown situation to work some of these out. But that first day, it became apparent that having Louise in the same apartment was not going to work.

To begin with, we had different sets of values on matters such as cleanness and tidiness. The Provincetown friends who began to drop in on us that day looked to Louise like hippies; the flat soon became a centre for our friends who did not for the most part belong to a conforming community. While Louise looked askance, or I felt she did, at our entourage, I was finding it difficult to watch her handling the baby along different lines from those I would have chosen without doing something about it, which I felt unable to do.

The main problem, though, was that of double authority: who was in charge of the boys, Mother or me? This was particularly a problem in relation to Billy, who made the most of the situation by embarking on the age-old game of 'playing off Mummy against Daddy', with myself cast, in this case, as Daddy. Louise was anxious to be cooperative and there were no battles between us, but the ambivalence of a situation in which there were two authority figures using different methods could only be confusing to the boys – for whom, after all, we were both there.

So I said to Mimi, 'We must have a meeting.'

Momma stay! (by Mimi)
The three of us met and quietly talked in the kitchen over cups of tea while the children slept. Rachel explained the problem to Louise and told her that she thought it would be better if she and Abigail could have a separate household, far

enough away to be clearly distinct while close enough to allow for easy visiting. Louise agreed, reluctantly but without raising any objections. She had given over authority to Rachel from the beginning and she wanted what was best for her sons, but she must have felt that we were virtually telling her she was superfluous, useful as a mother figure but not personally worthy. And in those early days we did feel that the hooks on the doors, the kids being kept in nappies, the reliance on television to entertain them, were acts of villainy rather than desperate attempts to cope. None of this was said at our meeting; we spoke instead of 'conflict of authority'. The decision was agreed on, and we parted to get sleep for the next day.

Both Rachel and Louise were up early to look for another apartment. Though it was off season, many of the tourist homes were being spruced up and were not available to rent. Finally, one of Rachel's friends found a place, a one-room apartment about fifteen minutes' walk away. Two assistants had joined us that day, Lorna and Wendy, and Louise was moved in Wendy's car.

Throughout that day we had been telling the boys, especially Bobby, that Momma would be moving to another house down the road. Bobby protested a bit, but it was not until Wendy started packing her car with Louise's things and the baby's that he finally realized that Momma was actually leaving.

Louise got in, her slim stylish appearance contrasting oddly with Wendy's casual clothes and ramshackle car. At once, Bobby started screaming: 'Momma stay!' at the top of his voice; he wanted to run after the car and we had to hold him back. Neither Rachel nor I had seen this clinging reaction to his mother before; in New York Rachel was used to his clinging to her in the foyer and running away from Louise. But Rachel had anticipated a scene of some sort. While Bobby screamed she repeated to him over and over again, 'I know you want your Mum, and I'm sorry, Bobby. She is going down the road to a different house and we'll see her tomorrow,' on and on until he had quietened down.

When Rachel and I were alone later, she reassured me that those terrible screams of Bobby's did not mean that the parting from his mother was causing him some harm, and clearly it hadn't, since he continued to progress. 'Traumas and separations are bound to take place in any childhood,' she explained. 'They may do damage if the child is in a non-caring environment, or isn't allowed to express its feelings. But Bobby is in a caring environment, with both you and me there to give him constant reassurance – in fact, instead of having to re-live the separation years later on an analyst's couch, as many adults do, he's been able to live it *fully* at the time, possibly re-living previous separation traumas too, with me there.'

She told me that fear and pain do not in themselves cause damage; screaming in itself is not traumatic. What is damaging is the kind of panic in which the deprivation is felt but not expressed. Had Bobby accepted his mother's leaving coldly, 'like a good boy', she would have been worried about him.

During those first two or three days I was finding it a real strain being with both boys, and could begin to see what Louise had been up against in that New York apartment. I was finding myself more at ease with Bobby; one of my best times with him was the night before Louise's departure, when I had taken a twilight walk with him to tire him (or me?) out, while Rachel bedded down Billy. We had had few battles; Bobby had chosen which directions we should take, stopping at phone booths for pretend lift rides and phone calls. His sense of direction was excellent, unless he could read my mind; he knew at which point we started heading for home, even after a walk full of turns.

But both boys together could drive me crazy; I longed for some tricks up my sleeve, or the wisdom to know which battles were worth fighting. I needed more work or thought on losing my temper, though at least my seeing red did not include hitting them; when they were being extra difficult my reaction was to move them or restrain them. I was glad when Rachel took over so I could go out and walk off some steam, wondering whether I allowed myself to go nuts because I knew she could cope.

I had a particularly hard time with Billy; I had not had much to do with him before and he was very different from Bobby. Bobby was purer somehow, doing things that tried my patience, but acting from his inner compulsion, not for any effect on me. Billy was always trying to trick you into giving him attention, and had worked out that he could gain attention by being 'naughty', a word Rachel never uses. He would often go limp when grown-ups tried to make him move or pick him up, turning to quicksilver in their hands. I think, too, that Rachel and I both saw him as the extra; Bobby was our main task and main interest, and Billy seemed the smaller problem and of less interest. Inevitably, Billy sensed this.

It was worse when they were both together. They were attracted by different things, usually in opposite directions. Billy tended to stay with me, wanted to please (or annoy) the adult; Bobby would be off, having no concern for the adult at all. If they both happened to be interested in the same thing, such as Doug's bicycle, they would be constantly squabbling over it.

The day after Louise moved out I took Billy and Bobby to visit her separately. Both visits were difficult, through no fault of Louise's. While I was there with Billy he stepped out of her door and found some paintbrushes soaking in turpentine on the hall stairway. Billy was one of those children who sample strange solids and liquids without discrimination; he came back a minute or two later, smelling of turpentine and announcing that he'd just had a drink! We fed him milk and water and bread to dilute it, but he didn't seem to have drunk much, and we continued our visit, which consisted of

Billy baiting Momma at every opportunity – teasing Abigail, bringing food out of the fridge, throwing magazines and anything else he could find on the floor.

If Billy started behaving like this when with Rachel she would simply recap it, saying, 'Now you're throwing things.' Billy's reaction then would be to go on throwing things, but in a different mood; no longer in defiance of the adult. Some very disturbed kids, Rachel tells me, need to go on throwing things until the place is in chaos, but in the case of Billy, once he saw that the adult was with him, he would soon stop needing to do it.

Louise acted like most mothers, however, by saying, 'No, don't do that.' Whereupon Billy would promptly move on to something else equally irritating, constantly on the run, getting Momma's attention and getting at her at the same time. The apartment she was in was newly decorated, very neat and clean, and Louise was afraid of damaging someone else's property. She kept protesting but didn't really do anything. Perhaps my being there was hard for her; I was Rachel's envoy after all, so she didn't want to get punitive, and didn't know how else to deal with him. As for me, I was on Louise's home ground and a very recent addition to Rachel's team, so I didn't do anything either.

Suddenly, Billy threw up. We could smell turpentine, and we rushed him to the bathroom and fed him a lot of milk and water. He seemed to be all right, but the moment we got home he threw up again on the carpet. I cleaned up the vomit and gave him some more milk, thankful it wasn't Bobby, who won't drink milk. Later when Rachel came in with Frank, a doctor friend of hers, I reported the incident; they examined him and said that I'd done the right thing and Billy would be all right.

Having recovered from that drama, I walked over later to Louise's apartment with Bobby. In her warm room he fell asleep after a little while. It was a slow evening, but Louise and I talked a bit, each in our shy way, and began making some contact, aided by wine and endless cigarettes; we had both suffered from Rachel's turning our apartment into a non-smoking area! I tried to translate some of Rachel's philosophy for her, but didn't really know enough to be of much help. Louise sheepishly showed me some detergent she had bought. Rachel is anti-detergent, believing that no one who uses it ever rinses their dishes properly afterwards. Louise and I giggled together like conspirators at the idea that anyone would think *we* wouldn't rinse soap off dishes.

When it was time to go I wrapped my jacket around sleeping Bobby and carried him out. In the cold night air he woke and immediately began to scream, 'Momma! Go back to Momma!' With hindsight, perhaps I should have woken him up before we left, but I hadn't wanted to make a scene. I didn't go back; having made the decision I felt I should keep to it firmly. I carried him, talking constantly in Rachel fashion: 'We're going back to our place and Momma will stay at her place and we'll see her again tomorrow.' He kept screaming and I kept talking; it was a quiet night and Bobby's screams echoed up and down the street. We passed several people on the way who asked what was wrong or said, only half-jokingly, 'Stop beating that kid!' Bobby was so hysterical that I couldn't reply to them.

That walk home was perhaps the first time I fully empathized with Bobby, ignoring outsiders, even the outsider of Mimi's ego. I was with him in his helplessness, anger and pain, not wishing he were different, not wishing I were elsewhere. We arrived home to a dark, empty apartment and his screaming continued for perhaps half an hour more, with additional mourning for the absent Billy and Rachel. I drew a bath and put him in it. That soothed him; the age-old warm water cure. He fell asleep soon after, so it was all over by the time Rachel and Billy came in with one of the new helpers, Lorna.

'Poor Mimi,' commented Lorna when I described the

walk from Louise's. But I needed no sympathy; in fact I felt that I had grown a bit during that walk. I hadn't lost my temper, and I hadn't wanted to run away.

After that we visited Louise pretty regularly and sometimes bumped into her when we were out with the boys and she with Abigail. But she was bored and lonely in Provincetown and wondered what good she was doing there.

Louise in Provincetown (by Louise)
Actually, I was not as upset at moving out as Rachel and Mimi may have thought. I hadn't really been looking forward to sharing an apartment with Rachel; she was a very forceful character, which I am not, and we had different ideas on just about everything as far as household management was concerned.

My chief concern was taking care of the baby, who was still very small; it was difficult for me to get supplies of nappies and formula for her, and Rachel's veto on detergent made it very hard to get her bottles clean. Rachel thought I was over-protective towards her and clearly disapproved of my not breast-feeding her. (I hadn't breast-fed the boys either; I had felt that bottle-feeding would give me more mobility with them, and there was no pressure on me at the hospital where they were born to choose either breast or bottle, though the staff were progressive in that they encouraged a lot more contact with the baby than most hospitals at the time.)

As far as the boys were concerned, Rachel was in charge, and I willingly stepped out of the picture. I knew that I was there as a kind of living security blanket for them, and that was my only function, so I tried to blend into the background. But I did feel that the baby was not part of this scene, and I was relieved to be alone with her.

It was difficult for me and Rachel to communicate directly with each other, we were just too different, and I think at that time Rachel thought me cold, with no proper mother feelings. In fact I cared about all my children very much and liked to be close to them, but with Bobby, it was difficult. When I held him and kissed him he was passive, seeming not to care one way or the other; I felt that his screaming, the day I moved out, was partly annoyance because he found it hard to tolerate any change of the established order, and partly because he knew I was his mother, and *should* be there, rather than needing me as a person.

By the time Rachel had first arrived on the scene, I was already feeling that nothing I did with the boys was right, and I could no longer trust my instincts with them. I was doing something wrong; I wanted to do the right thing, but didn't know what that was. As a result, I became sort of frozen, afraid to act spontaneously, and to Rachel and her team it may have appeared that I was uncaring.

Whatever the differences between us, however, I completely trusted Rachel with Bobby and Billy. I couldn't always understand what she was trying to accomplish in certain instances, but I felt she knew what she was doing, and I could see changes in both of them since she had started work with them.

One good thing was that, although he still wet his bed, Billy was by now almost completely toilet-trained. The process was not complete, but it had started the day Rachel sent him home without his nappies. Sometimes he still wet himself, particularly at night, but more often he would choose to use the bathroom. Like Bobby, whenever Billy does something it's because *he* decides to do it, and I think at Rachel's he decided to do it because he was on his own, and perhaps he wanted to try a bathroom in someone else's apartment. It was a real relief to have Billy out of nappies because I was tired of changing bottoms all day, and being surrounded by supplies of nappies for three people!

Billy seemed much happier too; he seemed to be becoming free of his brother's influence, less frightened of Bobby, and

was exploring things on his own without looking for someone
to show him what he ought to be doing.

Bobby, of course, was enjoying all the freedom of doing
whatever he wanted to do, which was what he had been
trying to do before. Most of the time he didn't say he was
going to do something, because he still wasn't speaking
much; he just did it while people followed him around without any interference.

The changes in Bobby were always subtle, but there were
enough for me to see that Rachel's method was working. In
New York he would come back after his Hours elated and on
a different plane, and would take some time coming down,
but I understood how Rachel's method was working with
him.

To some extent I tried to handle him the same way, but
I couldn't do that consistently because I still had to play the
mother-role and make decisions about allowing him to do
something or not – I couldn't let him run the house!
Sometimes he would come home extra agitated, or throw one
of his tantrums, and Rachel would tell me he had had a
breakthrough; I understood that sometimes things would
seem worse before they got better. I could never really
see immediate changes; with Bobby things just didn't happen that way. But I could see all the time that he was becoming more alive, less like a little self-wound mechanical
man.

Mimi I liked from the start; she was a quiet person like
myself and we seemed to get along well. The following week
at Provincetown we went out to dinner together and had a
very nice time, just being ourselves away from the children,
smoking and talking. Later on in New York she came to visit
us quite often and had dinner with us. She was able to act
very much as a link between Rachel and me, because she
understood what Rachel was doing, and could also see my
side at home. As I saw more and more of Mimi I felt a lot of
affection for her.

Rachel hires helpers (by Mimi)

Doug dropped in every few days, true to his promise on our arrival. He spent one afternoon with the boys and Rachel, patiently recapping as Billy and Bobby screeched at each other, squabbling over his bicycle. Each boy had one of the pedals and was trying to make it go round in the opposite direction to the other, thwarting each other and screaming, 'It's Bobby's! Billy go away!' '*No!* It's Billy's!' Doug spoke quietly, as one would with any rational people: 'These are designed to work cooperatively. Or you can prevent the other from turning the pedal if you stop turning your side.' He was calm, marvellous, his long legs folded under him, his curly head low, on a level with the boys.

Doug, of course, was trained in Children's Hours. I found such scenes exhausting, and made myself more exhausted by resisting instead of going along with events. At that time, although I was learning Rachel's methods fast, I wasn't willing enough to give of myself and I hadn't learned what Rachel calls 'the switch'; switching *off* oneself and *onto* the child. So I continued to get worked up, not giving vent to my feelings in the presence of the children, but taking myself out for a breath of sea air whenever everything got too much for me.

My life became a bit easier after three helpers were hired, Wendy and Lorna, who joined us the day Louise moved out, and Sam who was hired two days later. Rachel, as usual, interviewed all three briefly and set them to work right away. All three of them had been pre-selected by Barbara Baker, a friend and trusted former colleague of Rachel's, which assured their integrity. But it did not, as it turned out, assure their ability to fit in with Rachel's methods. Once someone is on Rachel's payroll she tends to forget that their training and life experience aren't the same as hers. Her patience with children is enormous; it is somewhat less with those she thinks of as her students.

Lorna and Wendy were both around thirty, and Sam was

younger, in his early twenties. Of the three Lorna fitted in with us the best. A pale young woman with glasses, who dressed fairly colourlessly, she didn't talk a lot but she gave of herself easily. She spent the most time with us, despite having some domestic problems of her own, and seemed to have a good understanding of what we were doing.

Wendy, stocky, olive-skinned and dark, went in shirt-sleeves while the rest of us were bundled up against the April winds; she had an air of competence about her which unfortunately crumbled while she was with us. She had a child of her own whom she was very fond of, so she always went straight home when her shift was over, and never joined in the talks with Rachel in the evening.

Sam was tall and rangy with long dark hair which he wore in a ponytail. He was somehow off his balance with us; he wore an intense look, laughed uneasily a lot, and didn't talk much, except at the wrong moments.

When they joined us Rachel gave them all a brief outline of the situation along the lines of: 'We have a problem kid and another kid, and we're getting them better. And what you've got to do is to be with one kid at a time, listen to it, be with it, let it do exactly what it likes. Let the child be the boss, and just take care of absolute basics – don't let him burn the house down, break your leg or anyone else's or annoy the neighbours too much. Normally you'd come in for fifty minutes, but this is a crash programme and we're working on an intensive basis, so you can start now and do the best you can!'

An arrangement was worked out so that there would always be two adults with the two boys; overnight shifts were included so that we could be sure of getting some sleep if the boys decided to be active at night. Lorna, who was very trade union conscious, wrote out a schedule of five-hour shifts. Rachel hated it and started ranting about it when she found it pinned on the wall. 'Five hours is not a day's work!' I think she would have had everybody working twenty-four hours a day if it had been humanly possible; all that mattered to her was to get Bobby better.

Rachel also introduced our new helpers to her work by having them as observers during an Hour. She gave Bobby an Hour the day after Lorna and Wendy were hired, and Doug gave him an Hour when Sam joined us.

7   Breakthrough in Provincetown

Bobby makes progress (by Rachel)
It had been clear from the start that my fantasies of a seaside
holiday were my fantasies, not Bobby's. The sea was the last
thing he wanted. But although Provincetown was not the
right choice of place, making the trip was the right thing to
do. During that first week Bobby had done a great deal of
living, and by the end of it he was already calmer, more
relaxed, more confident. We had uprooted him from his city
surroundings and we had sent away his mother. He had been
able to live through this separation, to express his anger at
me, and to grow through the experience.

On the following Monday an incident happened which,
though small, was significant enough for Mimi to note in her
diary: 'Rachel lies down and Bobby strokes her shoulder.'
This little touch, made as he passed me by, was not the kind of
thing Bobby normally did. It was not expressing a demand,
since I was asleep, and it was gentle enough not to disturb
me. It was a very pure gesture of affection and confidence.

Lorna had wondered during the Hour she recorded
whether we ever hugged or kissed each other: the answer is,
at that stage never. The desire for physical communication is
there in all children, but in Bobby it had been blocked. I for
my part hardly ever initiate physical contact with children; I
feel it is far too often forced on them by adults; most parents
do too much hugging and kissing, and it is best left to the
child to initiate this when he or she wants it.

On 18 April I gave Bobby an Hour with Sam as observer.
This was an extraordinary Bobby Hour. We went quietly for

a walk, and he was emotionally and physically quiet and relaxed throughout. He said, 'Bobby Hour.' I said, 'Yes, and Sam's coming, too.' So he took Sam by the hand.

When we came to the main road, I was half expecting a power struggle. I have a rigid rule that small children should take the adult's hand when crossing main roads – a rule that Bobby strongly objected to. Having discovered that the adult's danger sense was a very unreliable yardstick on which to base his behaviour, Bobby had settled for relying on his own danger sense; he often kept his hands in his pockets to avoid having them taken by an adult. Bobby's danger sense was uniquely his own, and I soon had to admit that it was distinctly superior to that of most adults. When I did get the message, painfully acquired, I cursed myself for being so slow to get it. Nevertheless, I would never deliberately allow a four-year-old – even Bobby – to cross a main road in my presence without holding my hand. So I said, 'I think "for real" we'd better have a hand over the road, Bobby.' ('For real' is the expression I use when I have to interrupt the fantasy world of the child's Hour with an important piece of adult information.) On this occasion, Bobby gave me his hand at once.

Then we had a little talk about 'for real' and whether he'd have a hand over the little road, and we compromised by him walking by the side of the road. But *he* wanted a hand sometimes, and he had it. There was no road trouble at all.

We went up several roads and Bobby talked to a lady in a car; he had rarely, if ever, chosen to talk to a stranger before. After that he wanted to call on houses; I said he could go down a step but we wouldn't knock at the doors because we didn't know the people. So he would just go down a step and come back again, and there was no battle at all.

We met a dog in a garden which Bobby wanted to go up to; a lady came out of the front door and said 'Can I help you?' So I just said, 'It's a Bobby Hour and he wants to talk to the dog. Is that all right? Thank you very much.'

In New York Bobby had been terrified of dogs, crossing to the other side of the road when he saw one, saying 'Doggie bite!' This desire to handle animals was quite new, and a sign of his developing sense of security. At one point Bobby started to go round a jeep into a garden and I suggested we didn't as we didn't know the people, and he accepted it.

On the way home he found a Siamese cat, also in a garden, the other side of a fence. He climbed over the fence and tried to lift up the cat, saying 'We'll go now!' to the cat. He eventually managed to get the cat through the hole, and petted it and kissed it. By the time he'd got the cat his Hour was over; he accepted it. I said, 'Your Hour's over now, and you're with Sam.' Sam brought him back and I went on ahead.

It was absolutely incredible. We had been here exactly one week, during which we had had Special Times with both boys. There had been a lot of power struggles over a lot of issues, but they had had such freedom for a whole week that now Bobby could have a calm, happy Hour like this.

His Hours in New York had been full of turmoil – 'Sorry, Bobby, you can't do that' – with violent upheavals as he pushed himself against barriers of all sorts, human, emotional, and physical. And this was an entirely new Bobby, talking reasonably and rationally.

I had done a lot of public relations over Bobby and now many people were coming up to us to say how struck they were to see these children changing. The ex-teacher upstairs, who had taken a special interest in him, and let him play with her typewriter, had expressed her amazement at how he'd changed, and a lot of other people had too. It was all very gratifying.

Fun and games (by Mimi)
I, too, was noticing the changes in Bobby. He was becoming much freer physically, more coordinated and less fearful. At first he would walk round the railings of our apartment

balcony to get to the beach, but after a while he was climbing over. We didn't play much on the beach, but that second week, one day when the tide was out I jumped down from the porch onto the sand below, about five feet. Bobby followed me. He was jarred by the fall and sank to the sand, but didn't start screaming as he would have done the week before. He dusted himself off, whimpering a bit, but saw that since he wasn't hurt there was no need to panic.

Piggy-back riding was something we started in Provincetown. I had always been amazed that he was afraid of it; although I knew he was not a normal kid I expected him to enjoy the things kids normally enjoy. Now, with lots of reassurance and the example of Billy, who had no such fears, Bobby first accepted a piggy-back ride, clinging tightly to his mount. Gradually he saw that the grown-up could be trusted not to drop him and he began to relax his hold and enjoy the ride.

Part of his fear may have been to do with his initial rejection of body contact. When I first met him he didn't want to be touched at all; I couldn't even take his hand or pat him. I am instinctively very physical with small children and although I didn't have any specific instructions from Rachel about this I saw it as an important thing for him to get comfy with. (Later she said that if it felt right to me then it probably was right, that I was now able to play these games with Bobby because he had grown to the point of being ready for them.)

Swinging him by the hands and feet was another thing that I initiated because he was so fearful of being carried or physically played with except with his arms around the grown-up, and theirs around him. At first he refused to be swung, barely allowing himself to be picked up. Billy was more at ease with this game, and once again Bobby took his cue from his younger brother. After a day or two of swinging they were both requesting swings whenever two grown-ups were present. So with Sam, Lorna or Wendy – sometimes all four of us with the two boys – it would be 'one, two, three and *down!* One higher, two higher, three higher – and *dump* him into the ocean! One, two, three – and *throw* him over the house!' Bobby began to love these standard play-threats.

It often seemed like the two brothers never played until we came into their lives. In fact they had one game that they taught us, an interpersonal game that went on to a greater or lesser extent the whole time we knew them. We called it 'Make happy, make sad'. Billy started it, and a step behind was Bobby. They would demand: 'Make happy!' and would get a smiling face in response. 'Make sad!' they said, and the reply would be an exaggerated mournful expression. The reply had to be in pantomime, and instantaneous. Later on they added 'angry', 'nervous', 'scared', 'freezing', and others, as they learned new words and concepts.

Usually it was just a fun game, the 'reply' being greeted with shouts of laughter from Billy even as he was giving the next command. Bobby's pleasure at the game was less demonstrative, though he requested it, so obviously he enjoyed it. But sometimes the game was a defence, an attempt to change the mood of a situation by the use of magic words. 'Make happy!' screamed Bobby at me one day in Provincetown when I was angrily shouting, and it broke the spell of the anger.

Our stay at Provincetown was the first time I'd felt relaxed enough to play with Bobby, and the first time I'd seen him play. He was growing more at ease and having more fun all the time.

Black Wednesday (by Rachel)
Everything seemed to be going beautifully – then it all happened.

Notes which I wrote at that time begin, regretfully: 'I have thrown Wendy away.'

What happened was this. It was Wendy's turn to take Bobby, and she was with him in the private beach-road outside our apartment, which contained the usual number of parked cars, as well as some in the process of parking and unparking. Of our three assistants I was least happy with Wendy. She was slow to grasp the basic concept of what we were doing, but behaved as if she knew it all; earlier on I had seen her cross the main road with Bobby without taking his hand, and once or twice I had found him on the far side of that road by himself. On this occasion I was not observer to the Hour, but was watching through a window. Bobby was running from car to car, trying the doors and quickly getting in, if he was lucky enough to find an open one. Wendy was running after him, trying to reason with him and he was not to be reasoned with. With mounting agitation, I watched her mishandling the situation.

Wendy had not grasped one of our basic Children's Hours rules, which is to prevent a child before it embarks on an action which is likely to be dangerous or annoying to the neighbours, not to stop it half-way through. All she had to do was to stand between Bobby and the object of his attraction and say, 'I'm sorry Bobby, I'm afraid you can't get in this car because the owner wouldn't like it.' By the time he was in the car it was far too late, and very difficult to get him out.

She had also made the error of allowing Bobby to climb up on the bonnet of her own car; this was confusing for him since in the absence of explanation, he assumed he was allowed to climb on the bonnets of all cars. Wendy stood by while Bobby climbed up on the car belonging to Katie, our landlady; Katie looked out of the window and shouted angrily, 'Get off that car!' whereupon Wendy took him down.

I ran out and took Bobby into a corner away from the adults to apologize to him for the mistake. I decided that Wendy should not be left in charge of him, and gave her Billy to look after instead. It was with Billy, however, that the last straw occurred.

Billy was standing at the side of the road behind a station wagon, and Wendy was on the other side, when Sam arrived.

Wendy broke another Children's Hours rule by taking her attention off Billy to say hello to Sam, just at the point when a large truck entered the cul-de-sac. When she looked back at Billy he seemed about to step out towards her and Sam, under the wheels of the truck, which he couldn't see. What Wendy did next was to dash forward and grab Billy out of the way of the truck. As she pointed out the next day, her action was instinctive and what most adults would do under the circumstances. And as I told her the next day, it was a highly dangerous thing to do. The effect of the panicky grab is to pave the path for the next accident, by taking away the child's sense of initiative and responsibility for itself.

In this kind of situation the adult has to control his own fear and grabbing instinct, as I had had to do with Bobby on the roof. The way to deal with it is to move over to the child quickly but with great calm, saying quietly, 'Watch it! There's a truck coming!' If it is absolutely necessary the adult can take away the child's control completely by lifting him up bodily, but still calmly. It is the half and half panic-grab that is so dangerous.

All of this I explained to Wendy the next day; what I did at the time was to lose my temper. I ran out of the house and gave her her notice. I had decided she was unteachable, and that I couldn't go on trying to teach her on real live material. I then retrieved Bobby from a car into which he hadn't been invited, and took him inside so that I could talk to him.

Doug and Mimi took Billy over, and I stayed with Bobby for the rest of that morning. After Wendy left, we went out again. He was angry with me because he had seen me lose my temper. He wanted to be on his own, at a distance from me, and he wanted to cross the main road. 'Rachel back house!' he repeatedly said. I kept my distance from him as far as I could while being near enough to take a hand when he got to the main road. When he did get there, he didn't want to cross, however; he stayed there investigating the cars, and finally lay down on the pavement, immobile.

It was at this point that Doug, Mimi and Billy came out of the house to go to the Post Office. They crossed over the main road and walked away on the far pavement. Bobby spotted them and immediately wanted to join them, particularly Mimi, to whom he was becoming very attached.

'Mimi!' he shouted, but Mimi didn't hear.

I was quickly by his side and offered him a hand, saying quietly, 'I'll give you a hand over the road if you want to join them.'

Would Bobby accept a hand over the road from me? Would he accept a dose of poison? He wanted to cross the road, Wendy had let him cross without a hand; he was determined to defy me and refused to compromise. He set about yelling, first in distress, then in the panic of rejection: 'Mimi come back! Mimi come back!' By this time Mimi herself was out of earshot and had no idea what was going on.

Bobby kept up his yelling for about half an hour at the top of his voice. Eventually he lay down again on the curb, almost under a car, and appeared to drop off into a sleep of agonized exhaustion. By this time all the folk in the vicinity knew beyond any doubt that Bobby wanted Mimi to come back.

Then the owner of the car turned up. He turned out to be an old acquaintance with whom I was on good terms. He said, politely and gently, 'I would like to use my car, please.' My gratitude to him was great for not attacking Bobby directly, as many a car owner would have done.

Bobby had no intention of moving from under that car. I had to get him out forcibly by pulling him by the hair. Sometimes you have to use force with children; but hitting them can of course be damaging, both physically and mentally. I have found that, for me, hair-pulling is the most undamaging and unviolent way of using force when force is necessary. In Bobby's case I had to use it quite often, and it never hurt him; in fact not feeling ordinary pain is one of the symptoms of autism. But it looks terrible to the onlooker, of whom there were several on that occasion.

Eventually the party including Mimi returned, Bobby was re-united with her, and I angrily issued instructions that in future no one but Mimi, Doug and myself should take Bobby.

I had further problems that day. While I was still alone with Bobby, Sam came up and told me that he was thinking of leaving, saying that he was feeling uncomfortable. Still shaken from the scene with Wendy, and very aware that I was 'with' Bobby, I answered: 'I don't care a fig how you feel. It is the kids who feel. Look at what you are learning . . . Can you make yourself missing so that I can talk to Bobby?'

Reading these notes four years later, I am not surprised that Sam felt uncomfortable. The next note reads:

> I am very tolerant of kids, and very intolerant of students. My students have kill or cure treatment – the ones who stay are wonderful but we have many casualties. I reckon folk should learn and learn fast . . . Folk find it hard to understand that we focus on the kids 100% – no time for concentrating on adults . . . This is the hardest job I've ever undertaken but a lot is coming of it.

In the afternoon Mimi took Bobby and I began to reflect on my own behaviour. In fact, the more I looked back the more awful I felt. That night I lived over the day's events in my head.

I had interfered and made Wendy lose confidence; I should not have done it at the time. I had been wrong to lose my temper when she reacted dangerously to the truck; so that there were two people out of control instead of just Wendy. I recalled Bobby's screams and saw myself as the inflicter of agonizing grief in a child whom I was claiming to help. I had remained calm and distanced while he yelled his head off. I was aspiring to the heights and had hit the depths.

The next day Bobby had a breakthrough.

As I have said before, I am incapable of explaining a breakthrough in scientific language. It is an occurrence so dramatic and so obvious that it defies definition, at least by me. The Bobby staff noticed it. The neighbours noticed it; instead of the hostility I had been expecting after our public display, I was greeted by, 'How did you do it? What has happened? That isn't the same boy.'

I realize now that it would have been a simple matter to hand around a questionnaire to our neighbours and obtain a written record of what they observed. But I didn't do any such thing. A breakthrough exists. It is poetry, not science; it is God, not logic; it is real. All I wanted was to tune into growth, and glory in the beauty of the organism that was Bobby, expanding and developing in his newfound freedom.

The next day I made time to talk at length with both Wendy and Sam. Although I had fired her, Wendy turned up for work as usual, but after a quiet discussion we both agreed that she was not cut out for this kind of job. She already knew where she had gone wrong. I apologized for interfering and losing my temper, and we parted on good terms.

Sam was a different matter. He was puzzled and confused, and wanted to leave. I didn't want him to; we needed a full quota of helpers and he had been doing all right on the whole. However, I had been too quick to tell him where he was going wrong, and he was suffering, among other problems, from a deflated ego.

He told me that over the last few years he had been learning to get in touch with his emotions, and now he was being told to switch off! He felt hurt because I appeared not to want to talk to him: this was because he was in the habit of trying to have little chats with me while I was 'with' one or both of the boys, either about his feelings or on the level of 'Did you have a nice walk?' When I am with a child, my attention is totally focused on that child, and adult interruptions at those times meet with a curt response. Sam's feelings were hurt.

There were a lot of other things that were puzzling Sam. All three of our helpers had been trained at the local counselling centre and they had probably arrived with preconceived ideas that didn't fit in with my methods. Sam hadn't yet grasped the role of taker, although he had observed Hours and talked at length to Doug. He couldn't understand what he was meant to be doing. 'I just feel I'm following them around making lots of mistakes,' he said plaintively. He was uncertain about how to set limits on the boys' activities and what limits to set; he hadn't understood my fury with Wendy when she grabbed Billy away from the truck, and seemed to be under the impression that I had intended Billy should learn about accidents by getting run over! He did understand after I'd explained it to him. He didn't know what was wrong with Bobby or what his previous history was; what was he meant to be observing?

I told Sam that the sink-or-swim method I use with my students is partly a defect of mine, because I want to get on with the job. But it is also partly deliberate; you will only look for and learn the answer to a problem when that particular problem arises, so I don't like filling people up with a lot of theory beforehand. Under my haphazard method there are as many who swim as sink; Lorna was a swimmer from the beginning, as was Mimi.

As for what was wrong with Bobby, I told him: 'You're not supposed to know. In this work it doesn't matter what's wrong, you deal with the kid exactly where he is. No, I don't want you to observe or look for any particular behaviour, though it's good if you keep records.'

I had made some headings to give some guidelines to Sam and anyone else who wanted them.

We went through them together, and this is what I told him:

1. LIMITS: There are very few limits, but those that are set must be rigidly enforced. We had to develop limits in

Toronto, including house rules, because we had seventy-five kids around and our workers included an army of dedicated young men who were excellent at their job but so concentrated on the children that they weren't concerned about what happened to the building or what the neighbours might think! As I was responsible for both the building and public relations, setting limits became important. The ones that were most important there were:

a) THE-HAND-OVER-THE-ROAD RULE. This must be enforced with small children. Even if a child says, 'But Mummy lets me!' I say, 'OK, but with *me* it is hand-over-the-road.'

b) Food stays in the kitchen and nowhere else.

c) Discretion must be exercised about the public – for example whether to let Bobby enter other people's doors, bearing in mind that we have another four days here and hope to return later!

2. HOW TO ENFORCE LIMITS: Apart from the above, limits have to be set according to what the taker feels he or she can handle, but they must be clear. If you, Sam, say it's OK for Bobby to go upstairs to look at the telescope, then that's your responsibility; don't bring him down after he's gone up. If you decide not to let him, then prevent it before it starts. Stand in front of the stairs and say, 'I'm sorry, Bobby, but I can't let you look at the telescope because it's valuable. I'm very sorry Bobby . . .', repeating it until you've got through to him.

3. SWITCHING YOURSELF OFF: Sam's personal needs have no place here, except in between Hours or in the evenings when the adults meet to talk. Or when, as you have now done, you make an appointment to see me, and I can then give you my full attention. When with the kids, Sam is *out*. So are other adults – you don't take your eye off the child if you bump into a friend in the street; you tell them, 'I'm sorry, I'm with Bobby.'

4. LAYING A MORAL TRIP ON THE CHILD: By this I mean

making the child feel guilty. It's when you say, 'Now, you know you're not supposed to do that,' or 'Now, eat up that nice pudding that Mummy has gone to such a lot of trouble to make for you,' or 'Be a good boy, just to please me.' In an Hour or Special Time the taker frees the child by assuming responsibility for adult values, and if there is an accident you apologize to the child: 'I'm sorry, Bobby, I let you spill the milk,' 'I'm sorry I didn't prevent you from climbing on Katie's car.'

5. LAUGHING AT CHILDREN: You should never laugh at a child when it makes a totally serious child remark. You may think it's cute or funny; to the child, to be received with laughter when it is perfectly serious is completely devastating. Imagine a poet reading his deeply-felt work out in public and being greeted by a chorus of laughter; that's what the laughed-at child goes through!

Sam interjected that he felt he had been laughing with the child, not at him. 'If in doubt,' I told him, 'see whether the child is smiling.' I went on:

6. CALLING THE CHILD'S NAME: I've noticed that you, Sam, like many other adults, tend to begin every sentence with: 'Bobby! Shall we do this?' 'Billy! Let's do that!' What this name-calling really means is: 'Bobby (or Billy), stop what you are doing and attend to me.' It is taking them away from where they are and drawing attention to yourself. A kid like Bobby takes no notice anyway, and good luck to him! Billy, with his anxiety to please, does, and I regard this as an affront. You have promised to give the child your attention, not take it away onto yourself. You can suggest activities by saying, 'Maybe we ought to be going out now.' This gives the child the option of paying attention to it or not.

7. CANDY IS OUT: In my view, sweets are the heroin of kids; they are what grown-ups give children instead of love and attention.

8. DOMESTIC CHORES MUST BE DONE QUICKLY: One of the perhaps less important things about this work is that all actions must have split-second timing. What is appropriate now is not appropriate in fifteen seconds from now. So all adult activities must be done at top speed. Anything like cooking must be done long before the meal, so that when 'food' is appropriate, 'food' can happen in thirty seconds; a disturbed kid does not understand time lag.

Of course, this doesn't only apply to disturbed children. I remember one mother being very grateful to me when I pointed out that she could do things like housework and food preparation at times when the child was not around. It hadn't occurred to her before. She had been trying to do things in the traditional way while two small, screaming children nearly drove her up the wall. She was delighted when I showed her that a meal could be got ready beforehand and then prepared in half a minute.

At the end of our talk Sam had a much better idea of what we were trying to do, but he told me it was extremely difficult for him to cut himself off, and he wasn't sure if he was right for this work. I pointed out to him that if we lost two helpers it was going to be very hard on those who were left. Sam was not going to be pushed into anything, and said he would sleep on it.

Having slept on it, Sam decided to stay.

Wet beds and dry pants (by Mimi)
Like Rachel, I find it hard to describe Bobby's breakthrough after that tense Wednesday. He still behaved in his own entirely individual fashion, but he was subtly changed, enough for anyone who had observed him to see the change. He held himself a little differently, a little more loosely, and moved with more grace. His face was not so intent, his mouth not so pursed. He screamed less and had a speck more patience; he was more at ease. The most specific change, however, was that he began to use the toilet.

Rachel had been right about plasticking the boys' beds; they were wet every morning. According to her, they were already in control of their bodily functions but because they had been kept in nappies they had been *taught* to wet their pants and the bed and needed time to unlearn the habit. Billy was a fast learner, but Bobby was taking his time about it.

The day after 'Black Wednesday' Bobby curled up on my bed in the afternoon and Rachel said I had better plastic it for the night; this time something told me she was right, and I did.

That evening I was sitting on Billy's bed while the two boys were playing quietly on Bobby's bed. Bobby started to pee but stopped himself: he got down and went out of the room into the toilet where he continued to pee in the proper place. His summons to me of 'Mimi!' was not his usual anxious call: when I arrived he was smiling in a quietly triumphant way, with the air of someone who has accomplished a small task, but accomplished it to perfection. Billy and Lorna also arrived to witness the deed and praise the doer.

That night Bobby announced that he was sleeping in my bed: 'This is Bobby's bed – Mimi sleep in Billy's room!' So I slept in Bobby's bed, and in the morning he had wet mine. So my bed became not my bed, and Rachel was proved right over the plastic issue.

Bobby was getting very close to me at the time, encouraged by Rachel who knew she would not be in the States forever, and I wondered if there was any special significance in his wanting to sleep in my bed. Rachel didn't think so; she said it was a normal part of childhood, a combination of play and curiosity about what it was like to sleep in an adult's bed.

After that, Bobby nearly always used the toilet for urinating in, though I continued having to clean his bottom end and pants for a while. (Rachel opted totally out of this aspect of Bobby care, and of clothes-washing.) For some reason, though, it was Lorna who Bobby asked to accompany him for each toilet pee.

Life over the last few days in Provincetown was more pleasant and even at times relaxed. Both boys were easier to handle now, though I lost my cool one day when Billy wouldn't stop screaming. On the last Saturday Doug gave Bobby an Hour which was quite different from any of his previous Hours. It was specifically concerned with fire-play.

Playing with fire (by Rachel)
Fire is one of the elements and children need to play with it as much as with the other elements of earth and water. Fire is essential play material, but it is dangerous – very dangerous; if not properly handled, the child and the public may get hurt. Yet the more fire is regarded as a forbidden, dangerous thing the more the chances are that children will get hurt by it; its forbiddenness makes it attractive, and at the same time they get no chance to learn how to handle it. Fire-play should be available to children all the time, if possible, under supreme supervision. In this way they get to learn the limits at the same time as fulfilling a basic need.

Doug and I had a good deal of experience with fire-play in Toronto; even there we didn't feel that everyone was able to deal with it. It was extremely therapeutic. I remember one child, a gentle, loving little boy who played with fire for months. He was very skilled; he was a scout and knew what he was doing. In keeping with our policy of not knowing the child's previous history, it was a long time before we learned that he had watched his dying mother being taken away in an ambulance after his father had shot her. Fire-play was what he needed in order to get over that terrible experience.

Here is Mimi's record of Bobby's fire-play Hour.

NAME: Bobby   DAY: Saturday
TAKEN BY: Doug   DATE: 23 April 1977
RECORDED: simultaneously by Mimi   TIME: 11 a.m.

Bobby walks around living room skips and jumps, stomps, followed and imitated by Doug (like a game of follow-the-leader). Goes into kitchen and gets wood. Lights (gas) stove jets. Match – burns fingers. Wood. Says to Doug: 'Fireplace. You do.' (Meaning that Doug lifted him to reach the gas-stove and the fireplace, which was fitted about four feet up on the kitchen wall.) Lights wood at gas jets. Carefully carries burning wood to fireplace. Back to stove. Lights candle with burning wood lit from stove. Blows out. Tries again to light candle. Drops charred end of wood and stomps it out. Takes stick to gas jet, turning burner with stick. Puts burning stick in broiler pan. Leaves it. Paper – lifts. (i.e. Bobby was returning to his earlier routine of playing at elevators.) Takes my hand. 'You do.' Gives me pen.

I was not present during this Hour. I recently re-read Mimi's account of it with a friend, who remarked that she found something very beautiful in the picture of this little boy carefully carrying fire around the room; that it seemed like some kind of sacrament. I can't better this comment.

Doug also made a note at this time: 'After the Hour, Doug is talking to Lorna. Bobby, on the floor by Doug's feet, urinates on Doug's right shoe. Doug says, "You peed on my shoe!" Then Bobby says, "Try the other one," and he pees on the left shoe.'

This seems to have been a demonstration by Bobby of his delight that he could now decide where to urinate. It was also an expression of affection for Doug, and indicates a sense of humour in Bobby which until then had only been latent.

Bobby was thoroughly enjoying his newfound control over where he urinated. He wanted to pee outside in some places where it was all right to do so and some places where it wasn't, such as making a parabola from the pavement aimed at oncoming traffic, and down the steps of houses. He accepted my prohibitions with little difficulty; in any case he liked to use the toilet, experiencing his new pleasure to the full.

The next day, our last in Provincetown, Bobby had another remarkable Hour. It was as if he wanted to use his time there as creatively as he could. The Hour was set up for the benefit of one of our neighbours, Elfie, who wanted to know what we were doing. At the start, Bobby didn't in fact particularly want an Hour and I persuaded him to have one; not something I would recommend as a rule.

NAME: Bobby   DAY: Sunday
TAKEN BY: Rachel   DATE: 24 April 1977
RECORDED: by Mimi   TIME: 10 a.m.

Discussion whether to have an Hour. Rachel weasels in and persuades him. Bobby at the window talking *out*. Speaking to Rachel, says 'Hi, Mimi!' Recognizes mistake and says so.

Cuddles with Elfie. Empty toy box. Wants blanket – cuddles with himself in chair. Quiet. Picks up bolster, unzips it, plays with it, places on bed. 'Stay right here.' Wants to go upstairs. But runs in other direction. Rachel goes out, Bobby says, 'Stay in.' She comes back in. Bobby says 'Hour is over.' (It wasn't.) Bobby invites in other kids, Elfie's Tom comes in. Rachel explains that it's Bobby's Hour. Gets a hug from Tom. Bobby wants to wear Rachel's watch and key (worn on a chain). Rachel arranges it. He puts it on, in Rachel's manner, walks like Rachel. Turn-about, *he* is the taker, as he has the watch. He says, 'Rachel's Hour is stop it.' He takes out watch, talks like Rachel. 'Rachel go.'

A whole lot of things were happening in this Hour, some more significant than others. Firstly, Bobby's need to cuddle was coming to the surface, which was good; in fact he seems to have put cuddling into the atmosphere, since Elfie's son Tom came in and cuddled me. Secondly, inviting in other kids was extremely unusual for Bobby: during this Hour this solitary boy became a social animal. I should say that this act of socialization was not followed by an immediate permanent change; outside Hours Bobby did not usually choose to relate to other children, but he was demonstrating that the potential was there.

Bobby's imitation of me was very interesting. The whole essence of taking an Hour is that the adult 'becomes' the child by going along completely with the child's actions and needs. Now here was Bobby pushing out the boundaries of his personality and taking control of events by 'becoming' me. In a sense he had been 'becoming' Mimi when he slept in her bed. 'Rachel's Hour is stop it!' was good speech for him at that stage.

All of these things: cuddling, sociability and imitating me, showed enormous developments in Bobby's hitherto limited emotional behaviour.

And then it was time to go. The return trip seemed much smoother and shorter. With the memory of our exhausting outward journey still fresh, we took Lorna with us so that there was always one adult off duty.

We drove to Provincetown Airport in two relays, so Bobby and I had to wait for a while in the exit lounge. There, a nice official let Bobby into a control room full of switches and enormous electric typewriters. I had visions of total air chaos resulting from Bobby's activities, but the man just said, 'Leave him to me, he's all right,' and let Bobby loose turning switches; perhaps the man had turned off a master switch. I thought it funny that an official should tell *me* to let Bobby do as he wanted, and apparently it was all right as there were no mid-air crashes or other disasters that day.

We flew to Boston in a smaller, eight-seater plane; a grown-up passenger took the front seat so there was no conflict over whether to give Bobby a turn next to the pilot. He protested at first, 'Bobby be in front seat,' but he didn't persist. Instead, he and Billy plied us with questions. 'Where are we going? Where's Provincetown? Where's Daddy?'

When we arrived at Boston we split up, as Louise and Abigail were flying home while we took the train again. It was an easy parting; though we were leaving their mother, Bobby and Billy were reassured that we would meet up again at home; and besides, we were going on the train! Meanwhile, Bobby made his impact on the airport staff by succeeding in turning off one of the escalators.

We were half-way home on the train, when Lorna and Bobby came into the car where Mimi and I were sitting, she smiling and he looking mysteriously triumphant. Lorna reported that Bobby had shit in the train toilet.

Mimi and I congratulated him warmly, but our approval was superfluous to Bobby, whose achievement was deeply in the past; he said, 'Come on Lorna!' and moved on to the next activity.

We were pleased, but not surprised. Bobby had been growing more comfortable in his body all the time we were in Provincetown, and the use of the toilet came when he was ready for it. It's interesting, though, that Lorna was the one he chose to be with him, not myself, and especially not Mimi, who was the primary bottom-wiper, and would be for some time to come!

All in all, we had gained a great deal from the trip to Provincetown, despite the fact that in taking Bobby there I had behaved as a typical adult. I had correctly collected from him the message, 'I need some space,' but I had most incorrectly interpreted the nature of the space he needed. I had superimposed my concept of my own childhood's country space onto Bobby's obvious preoccupation with late twentieth-century press-button urban space. Looking back on it now I marvel at how I could have made such an error. I had been practising and teaching Children's Hours for about fifteen years; I was never tired of reiterating, 'Follow the child, initiate nothing.' And yet I took him to a non-urban space.

There may come a time when Bobby needs his 'forty days in the wilderness'. This time will come, I would suggest, when he has had his fill of human relationships and communication with his fellows. At the time of the Provincetown trip, because of his inability to communicate he had been starved of human relationships and was hungry to relate to people. The long, contemplative silence of communicating with himself and the God within him lies well into the future.

At the end of those two weeks Bobby still could not look an adult in the eye, he still darted away like a bullet if he sensed any intended intrusion into his self-contained life. He still rang every front doorbell and opened every door that would open. In short, he was still autistic and recognizable as such by professionals. To those unaware of his condition he was still 'an undisciplined little brat who needs his backside spanked'.

Nevertheless, Provincetown was a landmark from which Bobby never looked back. Although strangers were still objects to be manoeuvred, and his emotions were still largely locked up, he had accepted and shown affection to a number of new people. He had begun to use the toilet. He had learned to play, both with others and by himself. Bobby had started to enjoy being alive.

8 Back in New York

We wear labels and red sashes
After our return to New York we all had a couple of days off
to recuperate, and Lorna went back home with our thanks.
The day I resumed his Hours, Bobby got lost for the first
time, and by no means the last. Up until then he had spent
most of his Hours with me in the building, on the lifts, on the
roof, and in the lobby pretending that the telephone boxes
were lifts.

The new hazard occurred when Bobby said, 'Rachel stay
here and Bobby go in the lift.' I had to do some very rapid
thinking: would he come back or go out in the street? Which
hotel staff member would he meet and what would their
reaction be to him and to me? Which staff member was on
phone duty in the lobby?

Real danger and damage had no part in this list. Bobby,
even in those early days, was totally to be trusted in those
two fields and, as I was discovering to my surprise, was well
able to take care of himself in traffic.

Having decided to comply with Bobby's request that I
should stay alone in my apartment while he went on his
travels, I sat down and waited. Time went by. The waiting
seemed too long. I made enquiries in the lobby and was told
he had been seen leaving by the front door some twenty
minutes before.

I had so far kept out of the way of the desk staff, as far as I
could, in my dealings with Bobby. I had tried to explain the
work to those I felt would understand, and had left a copy of
Dibs for general circulation; I was eventually given it back,

and was given to understand many had read it, but neither they nor I had followed this up. Many of them were helpful, but on this day the girl on duty had watched Bobby walk out of the building and had not thought it worth informing me.

I phoned the police and gave a description of Bobby as best I could. I am very non-visual and notoriously unable to describe even my nearest and dearest. I made a note then that I would ask Louise to supply me with a description of his age, height, hair-colour, clothes, etc., ready for use should there be any further losses. Having phoned the police I went outside to wait for them. I was anxious that my landlord should not see me with them in the lobby, though I discovered later that he was perturbed about Bobby's loss and wanted to be cooperative.

I did not succeed in keeping the police out of the hotel lobby. Quite soon Bobby was decanted out of a police car with a look of ecstasy on his face. I thought how uncorrupted are the values of children and the memory came to my mind of a two-year-old I took to hospital in an ambulance many years ago. On arrival he sobbed so intensely that all were puzzled, as his mother was still with him and there appeared to be no other obvious cause for the tears. Eventually out through the tears came, 'I want to go back in the big white motor-car!' A generation later, the son of this child, then aged about three, was in the care of his grandmother when she was arrested. He witnessed the incident, which was done with concern by the police, who made sure that the child was safely in the care of another family member. The child was nonetheless extremely upset; eventually he gave the reason for his distress – *he* wanted a ride in a police car too. To neither generation of children did the ramifications of either hospital or arrest mean a thing. What they quite clearly wanted was to ride in a big white motor-car and in a police car. Bobby was no different.

There was no difficulty with the three policemen: they just asked a few questions and satisfied themselves as to my identification. One of them I was to meet again when Bobby got lost later; he remembered Bobby and showed interest and concern for his progress. On this first occasion, they advised me to sew Bobby's name and address inside the back of his coat. From that day on, Bobby was labelled, not on the inside of his coat, but with a label pinned or clipped on to his pocket or front, clearly to be seen. It always surprised me that Bobby never resented his label or tried to pull it off. He seemed quite fond of it and treated it rather as folk do a favourite hat, scarf or pair of gloves, as an extension to his personality.

The actual wording of the label varied. If written by Louise it was neat, factual and circumspect, attached by an elegant clip. If written by Mimi it was somewhat impulsively worded, usually attached by a functional safety pin. If worded by me, it could contain anything from basic minimum facts to barely legible comments according to my mood. On one occasion I remember Louise making a mild protest when I wrote, 'My name is Bobby. I am quite safe. If worried or Bobby appears lost, phone . . .' She suggested that perhaps it was not quite true to say he was quite safe, so I altered the wording, omitting it.

Soon after the label-wearing had started, it became apparent that labelling Bobby was not enough; it was also necessary to label the 'takers', by making ourselves spectacular in some way. The way I chose was for the adults to wear a wide red ribbon sash and a label, and for Bobby to do the same. The reason for this was that Bobby would often be a long way away from his taker, perhaps at the far end of a subway platform. If the public spotted Bobby's apparent lack of an adult in charge and started looking around to see if there was such a person before taking action to rescue him, it was easy for the taker to raise a hand, pull at the sash and give a reassuring sign, indicating, 'He's OK, he's with me.'

The sashes were not accepted easily by everybody. Some of them felt uncomfortable and several protests were made.

It is true that in the early days they were just torn frayed pieces of red material, and were anything but elegant. Even when Mimi had succeeded in creating a secure, more elegant sash, many of the team and observers were reluctant to wear it. If I were to embark on a similar project now, I would have team and children dressed in identical tee-shirts.

I also made arrangements with the desk staff that if they saw Bobby going out of the door they would ring me on the intercom right away.

Back in New York (by Mimi)
After our return from Provincetown, Billy, now fully house-trained, started going to a nursery, a small private school, more liberal and progressive than most free city schools. He was delighted; he was ready for some structured time with other children, out of his brother's shadow. And Bobby resumed his daily outings with me. With a sinking feeling I saw that he was going to continue playing with the same 'toys' as before our trip. He may have begun to speak more clearly and use the toilet, but he still wanted to push buttons, especially escalator emergency turn-off buttons. And he still wanted to go on interminable subway rides and explore all manner of strange places. The shy part of me recoiled from always having to PR the public and the grown-up part of me resented taking orders from a kid. But with encouragement from Rachel, and my own sheer stubbornness, I kept on trying to see things through Bobby's eyes.

As Rachel was due to go back to Los Angeles for a month to fulfil her obligations there, she hired a young man named Richard to assist me in her absence. Slender, slight and self-effacing, he was not the sort of assistant I would have picked. He was friendly, and could learn from experience, but could not initiate action.

Richard and Bobby and I got into a sort of routine, riding the elevators in Bobby's home building and adjacent apartment buildings, going on to Woolworth's and Gimbel's nearby to ride the escalators. Richard and I tried outflanking Bobby to keep him away from the shin-level turn-off buttons, often succeeding but sometimes not. He'd dash between people, change direction, arrive on another floor ahead of us, press a button and quick as a wink the escalator would grind to a halt. Bobby would be off with one of us in hot pursuit and the other off to find the store manager with a key to restart the escalator.

Gimbel's is a huge store, with eleven floors, so we rarely ran into the same manager twice, and were unable to do any lasting PR. Later, after consultation with Rachel, we would remove him from the place if he did stop an escalator. We would apologize to him and tell him we were sorry to stop his fun but we also made it clear that what he did was not allowed. We never said he was bad or naughty, and we never related what was going on to past action, nor made threats for the future; but in the present, it was not allowed.

Bobby alternatively shrieked, pleaded and dragged his feet to stay – he so loved that place with its moving stairways! But having made the decision, we kept to it and left even if it meant carrying him. Once on the street, the episode was usually forgotten as we went on to whatever was next. Rachel meanwhile, went to PR Gimbel's.

Gimbel's (by Rachel)
I soon realized that Bobby was being very inconveniencing to the store, and learned that there was a long history in the past of his mother having trouble with him there. So I went to see the management. I gave them *Dibs* and our literature, talked to them and asked for their cooperation because, as I told them, if we went on coming to the store, occasionally an escalator would be turned off. We would try to avoid this, but if it did happen, please would they let us handle it? They were extremely cooperative and understanding. The manager said, 'All I ask is, please let us know if you're in the store,' which I agreed to do.

I really appreciated Gimbel's cooperation. It was a store that Bobby loved to visit and which his mother had taken him to in an agony of 'Don'ts!' It was very good for him to be able to return as a welcome guest to a place where he had been an unwelcome one and allowed, in moderation, to do what he needed to do.

Turning off escalators may strike some people as an odd form of therapy. Bobby, like all children, had a need to do things he could do, and at that time there were not many of those. Pressing buttons was one of them. By doing this he was learning to control his world and control his body, as well as fulfilling a desperate inner need. So we had to find buttons that he could press, like lift buttons, and prevent him, regretfully, from pushing buttons that would bring Gimbel's, or anywhere else, to a halt.

If I were a millionaire I would found a clinic full of escalators and lifts! Every child, and every adult indeed, needs to do the things he can do with approving adults around, so that he can grow to the next stage. If we adults could receive approval for our neurotic and compulsive behaviour instead of criticism or laughter, we, too, could eventually grow out of the need for such behaviour.

It was in Gimbel's that I first saw Bobby handle a toy. At first the merchandise in the shop, even in the toy department, was totally ignored by Bobby; his interests were lifts, escalators and movement, he didn't even see the other merchandise as toys.

There came a day when Bobby saw a small bus in the toy department. He stopped; he bent down; he handled it. I was on duty to accept all that Bobby did, so I had no right to be amazed. I quickly located the sales assistant and had my reassurance speech ready, should it become necessary to make it, though it seemed unlikely; I still marvel at the fact that Bobby did not damage things; but I was mentally costing the toy in the unlikely event of actual damage occurring. As far as possible I was explaining Bobby to the assistants and trying to allay their anxieties while, if possible, enlisting their support.

In the midst of all these thoughts and actions, I was elated to watch Bobby handle the toy; I hadn't previously seen it happen.

I should make it clear that we had no step-by-step goals for Bobby's development; he chose where he was going next and all we did was to go with him, supplying him, or attempting to, with experiences he needed. It was no part of our programme to 'graduate' him from lift buttons to toy buses. It was the newness of the interest that we welcomed; any new interest would have been welcomed in the same way, provided of course that it wasn't grossly anti-social. This was unlikely in Bobby's case, as he was not an anti-social child. He was a child hungry for education in its widest sense, and for good human relationships.

Mimi was helping him to discover both, and continued to do so after I had left again for Los Angeles, leaving an experienced Canadian colleague, Linda, in my flat.

Exploring New York (by Mimi)
During the first week of May, Bobby, Richard and I went to playgrounds, two schools and Robert's office, took the Staten Island Ferry, rode lots of lifts in stores and apartment buildings and travelled by subway, which Bobby loved. We'd spend four to five hours with Bobby, getting him home for supper.

Once Linda and I took Bobby to see *Star Wars* at the movies. We had the typical grown-up attitude about it – he had said he wanted to see that movie, so we interpreted that to mean he wanted to see the whole thing, as we did. Bobby watched the first quarter or maybe half-hour, then wanted to move around, then to leave. We took turns, one of us wrestling with him or talking to him in an effort to persuade him to stay seated, while the other watched the screen, grimly getting our money's worth. We succeeded in seeing the whole picture, but none of us enjoyed it.

I learned from that movie outing. A month or so later Bobby wanted to see *Orca – the Killer Whale*, which, like *Star Wars*, he'd seen advertised on TV. I had a spare four dollars that day, so I decided to take him and see what happened. We watched the screen a short time until Orca made his debut. Bobby got out of his seat and raced down to the front seats, first for a better view, then to run around yelling 'Orca!' at the other kids watching the movie. When it seemed that the other kids would rather watch the screen than Bobby, I made this known to Bobby, and gave him the choice of watching or leaving. As he had seen as much as he wanted, we left. So in one way the admission price was wasted, but in another he got out of it what he wanted. And since I had had no preconceived desire to see the whole film, I was calm about leaving it early.

Of course, except for Linda we were not giving Bobby formal Hours, and we all had our own limits. But I was beginning to learn to apply Rachel's methods to these Special Times. I was learning that a person who is tired, or afraid of something, or in a hurry to do something important, can say so to the child, taking responsibility for their wishes rather than foisting blame onto the child. Rather than telling him, 'You are wrong to want to do that,' you can say, 'I'm sorry, but I have to rest now,' or 'I'm sorry, but I can't let you explore the roof; I'm afraid of heights,' or 'I'm sorry, we can't linger here; the bus we're going to catch is the last bus tonight.' Apologizing is a necessary part of it, expressing that ideally you would like to go along with the kid, but since it is impossible you understand his disappointment. Kids know the sincere from the phoney. Knowing that he's understood is often enough to calm a child down; once he realizes that he's got through to you, he doesn't need to go on whining, nagging or otherwise trying to get your attention.

A few days after Linda arrived I wrote to Rachel in an optimistic mood:

Tuesday, 10 May 1977

Hi Rachel,
I heard your voice on your tape recorder, just saying 'Hi',
and got as excited as Bobby to hear it. He cried when he
rewound the tape and lost you though, and tonight I am
wondering if that was unusual, for him to cry – I thought it
was something new breaking through, but maybe not.*
I've never seen him cry before. He also cried (red face,
tears, dismayed shouting) today when Linda got off the
subway as our routes split, he and I to his apartment, she
to hers.

We went to the beach at Coney Island, Brooklyn for a
short time today and he started talking about Provincetown. The area bears a certain resemblance to it in the
layout of buildings and the beach beyond. We were eating
French fries and he started a litany with me; slowly at first
and more and more happily:

B: Where's . . . (unintelligible)
M: I beg your pardon?
B: Where's Sam?
M: In Provincetown.
B: Where's Lorna?
M: In Provincetown.
B: Where's Wendy?
M: In Provincetown.
B: Where's Rachel?
M: In Los Angeles.
B: Where's Richard?
M: In his room.
B: Where's Mimi?
M: I'm here.
B: Where's Linda?
M: Right behind you.

* I do think that this did represent a breakthrough in his ability to express
emotions.

And we all laughed; each question and reply was more fun than the last, completing the list of people who'd been his 'enlightened babysitters'.

Things go well. One unfortunate coincidence is our being out in the afternoons when, after eating or drinking, his bodily rhythms produce shits (3 times in 6 days). So we're back to packing extra clothes with us in our travels, and hopefully his bowels will start churning after breakfast or supper one of these weeks, rather than after an afternoon snack. Today on the beach I saw his face working and that characteristic stance and I said, 'Shit on the sand! Shit on the sand!' But a forced removal of his pants did not appeal to him at all. He shit in his pants and we more or less cleaned him up.

A couple of days ago we fixed up to go and pay a visit on Billy's school, which Bobby's been wanting to do for a long time. The principal was full of interest to see this kid she'd heard of. But she had other things to do, and so did Bobby, so it was brief. After half an hour or so of play among the other kids there and by himself, they were rounding up their crew for the start of the day, so we made to part. Bobby agreed to it rather easily, though Billy put up a fuss, wanting to go with us. His heart must not have been in it, though, as he did stay with the other kids and teachers without physical restraint.

We found a subway station full of escalators, whose turn-off buttons are up on the wall out of his sight and reach! Heaven for both of us. We are also coming across friendly elevator men in buildings on the east and west sides.

Linda had Bobby on her hip today, with Diane (an observer) standing nearby, during his Hour. He had them come face-to-face in a three-way hug, then said, 'Talk.' Linda said, 'You want us to talk to each other?' He said, 'Yeah.' They said, 'Hi.' Directing others to interact with each other, imagine!

Richard and Bobby were good together. One day Bobby had shit his pants at some distance from home. He wanted to be held on the subway and neither Linda nor I would hold him, because although he had been cleaned up he still smelled. But Richard's compassion overcame his sense of smell, and he picked the little boy up, giving him the body contact he wanted.

Even after Richard wasn't on the payroll any longer, he welcomed Bobby to visit in his room, which he shared with another young man. Bobby and I would go to Richard's door and sometimes Bobby would have me wait outside. Even if Richard's time was short he would allow a quick visit, and so Bobby had another friend to drop in on.

All in all, Bobby did not seem to suffer from Rachel's absence during that month. None of us had her talent for completely tuning in to him, but we gave him what we had. He grew more comfortable physically, touching us and letting himself be touched and held and tossed about. He began to respond to other children's approaches, in the Green School and in the public playgrounds. We even got flashes of eye contact, though he still never glanced up when his name was called.

Late in May, before Rachel came back, Bobby and I were with Linda and Billy at Battery Park, on the swings in the playground. Bobby could swing all day or as long as someone would push him, since he wouldn't propel himself. This was strange, because I learned later that the first time Bobby was put on a swing, he was immediately able to swing himself, which seemed very unusual in a child not yet two. As a variation, I was pushing from the front, by his knees, laughing with him as he would reach out to kick me and shouting at him to keep his feet back.

The playground was crowded, no other swings available, so Billy requested Bobby's swing. Bobby gave himself a countdown from twenty, and looked me straight in the eye for the whole count as he swung close to me, then away . . .

'4-3-2-1-A', after one of the lifts in his apartment building. At 'A', he popped off the swing.

It was the longest I had ever held his gaze. It was precious. I hardly blinked, as the rest of the world disappeared but for the dappled sunshine on the swinging boy with his eyes open at last.

9 *Subways and Buses*

Back from Los Angeles (by Rachel)
I spent a month in Los Angeles, as planned, but things did not turn out as I had hoped. There was no current programme in which I could work, and as time went on I realized that my dream of starting up a clinic similar to the one I had left in Toronto was not going to be fulfilled. I had talks, arranged discussions and gave demonstrations; the potential seemed good, but nothing other than good relations came out of it. It appeared that I was not destined to get my work going in Los Angeles.

While I was away I was quite happy about Bobby. I kept in touch with Linda and Mimi by post and telephone; Linda was giving him Hours and I was very pleased with the work Mimi was doing. She was much more directive than I was, but she was giving Bobby the attention he needed for his growth.

When I arrived back in my New York apartment, Bobby was my first visitor. As he came in he did something he had never done before. With a broad smile on his face he ran across the room to me and gave me a big hug.

Not long after my return, Mimi said to me, 'How much longer must I go on with Bobby on the subway? I'm getting tired of day after day on the subway!'

In the Toronto Clinic two years before, one of the workers who was taking David – the boy, who, we later discovered, had seen his dying mother being carried away after being shot by his father – had said to me, 'How much longer

145

must I go on playing "Bang, bang, you're dead!" with David? It doesn't vary. There's no creation in it. I've been doing it for months now. Is there no way I can suggest some alternative play?' We considered the question seriously. I said that we could suggest something different to David, but it would be against our overall policy and I personally would not be prepared to risk it. I suggested to the worker that she should bear it a little longer and if she felt she could not continue we would schedule David for a different taker. The very next day David started on a new activity.

Of course there could be many explanations of this, besides sheer chance. The worker may have conveyed her need for change to David by some gesture or attitude and David may have picked up the message and responded. He may have been ready for a change before she spoke to us and in some way conveyed it to her. The explanation I favour is that both of them were in tune with the approaching change.

In the case of Mimi, Bobby and the subway, no such change was to occur. We had a long talk about the situation. It was natural that Mimi should feel, and sometimes show that she felt, impatience at repeated activities. But there could only be one answer to her question. The only person to call a halt to any activity and embark on a new one is the child himself. The natural learning of a toddler is very repetitive. A happy fulfilled toddler does not need the full attention of an adult while he is learning. Bobby, who was emotionally anything but fulfilled, did. A toddler learning a new activity will repeat it endlessly, or apparently endlessly, to the adult in charge. Of course the activity is not endless; it is finite; it finishes when the child finishes it, provided that the child is still growing.

Bobby meets the public
Shortly after I got back from Los Angeles, Bobby was on a normal subway outing for this period. When we went out together he would dart ahead as soon as he spotted a subway

station, dart down the steps, dodge under the pay turnstile (small children don't pay fares in New York), and onto the platform. Sometimes, on arrival, I found that a train had arrived and Bobby was in it, doors shut and away before I could manage to join him.

I doubt whether Bobby ever got lost on purpose; he got lost because I was not quick enough to keep up with him. I never saw him use 'hide-and-seek' tactics in order to get rid of me, although he did occasionally use such tactics quite definitely because he wanted to go one way when I wanted to go another. This only happened on journeys home or other journeys with a fixed destination, because at all other times it was accepted that Bobby went exactly where he wanted.

The question of Bobby getting lost involved one of those calculated risks that must be taken when a disturbed child is on the road to health. I am told that similar getting lost incidents occur with English social workers in charge of deprived children; every time a child takes off they have to ask themselves: 'Do I allow my anxiety about the child to stand in the way of the freedom he needs in order to grow?'

Of course I was anxious when Bobby got lost. At the same time I had discovered by now that his traffic sense was phenomenal, and I knew what his reaction would be if approached by a child-molester. The typical kid-seducer will be smarmy to a child with sweets and smiles, and no way was Bobby going to be attracted by those sorts of tactics. Bobby was, and still is, completely direct, and could recognize lack of directness in others. He would have reacted as he always did to people he disliked, by screaming loudly, spitting and running away.

He was always found and returned to me within a relatively short time; three hours was the longest. His finders fell very clearly into two categories. First were concerned members of the public, ordinary people and very often social workers, who, finding him on his own, read his label and handed him in to the police, usually leaving their names and addresses; whenever possible I followed these people up. The second type of person was angry that Bobby should be on his own, and angry at what he was doing, because it looked dangerous, although it wasn't; they would almost throw him at the police, telling them to find his mother and do something about her. The police themselves, throughout America, were cooperative, kind and understanding, with one notable exception which came later, in Los Angeles. Bobby and I still talk about the Los Angeles policemen!

Every time, except in Los Angeles, that Bobby was returned to me in a police car he was radiant.

On most occasions on the subway I just made it in time to join him on the train, though not always in the same carriage. I would attempt to remedy this at successive stations, not an easy job, considering Bobby's skill at mingling unobserved in a crowd. I was glad about my decision to dress us both in red sashes.

On occasions when Bobby and I both arrived on the same platform at approximately the same time, we would ride the trains for as much time as I had available; we would get off when Bobby decided to and get onto another train when he decided to. I would sit as far away from him as I reasonably could both when on a train and on a platform; this distance from Bobby was the exact opposite from the closeness which is used in formal Children's Hours, but was totally compatible with the basic Children's Hours principle, since it was what Bobby wanted.

When I judged that we were about as far from home as would fill the time available to get back, I would say, 'Hi, Bobby, we must head for home now. Can you get us on the right train, please?'

Bobby would hear, understand and say nothing. I have never mastered the New York subways and usually had no idea of where we were, or how to get home. Sometimes Bobby's silence would last long enough for me to start feeling anxious, especially if we had a deadline to meet, but I soon learned that he switched on his home-going clock the moment I asked him to. Like a general on full alert, he was planning his retreat, and would act the moment he had finished formulating his plan. He would sometimes make a mistake and, again in expert military fashion, would immediately change course with no apology either to me or himself. He always got us home.

On this particular, never-to-be-forgotten day, I was sitting on a bench on an uptown subway station in New York City, probably in or near the predominantly black-inhabited district of Harlem. I was near one end of the platform; Bobby was right up at the other end. As was my custom I was explaining my activities with Bobby, and the reason for them, to the other seat occupants. They were understanding and interested as I waxed eloquent about Bobby, his past life, his potential for growth and our work in 'setting him free'.

'Here he comes,' said one of the women, spotting Bobby running towards us.

'Hi, Bobby!' from me; and then suddenly it came to me that I had to introduce him to the women. 'What's your first name?' I quickly asked the woman next to me.

'Elsa.'

'Bobby,' I said, 'this is Elsa. Elsa, this is Bobby.'

'Hi,' said Bobby. 'What's your name?'

'Elsa.'

'Hi, Elsa,' said Bobby.

He looked her straight in the face for a few seconds before going on to the next one. Exactly the same dialogue, with exactly the same, intense concentration on each new person was repeated four more times. Bobby gave each woman in turn a few seconds of full eye contact.

I had never seen him relate to strangers before this. Of all Bobby's numerous breakthroughs, this was the one that had me nearest to tears.

As well as the subway, Bobby loved riding the city buses. I see from Richard's reports that he was already 'helping old ladies off the buses' in May, so his bus activities must have started while I was away. They were to go on for a long, long time, and for several weeks the bus and all things inside and outside it, like the subway; in fact all things, ideas and people connected with them, were the centre of his thinking, feeling and acting.

Irresistible to Bobby were the yellow school buses. If he saw one with its door open or being boarded by a group of children he would dart into the road to board it too. On those occasions I sometimes wondered if a contributory motive was his desire to be a schoolboy and belong to the society from which he had been cut off for so long, but perhaps the attraction was just the bus.

There were times when Bobby would board a bus and firmly tell me to stay behind, go home, or go somewhere else. I felt really sad for him as I explained that I had to get on it with him because that was a bus rule. In his mind and in fact he was quite capable of travelling alone, and I felt awful at having to intrude and interfere with his freedom. How I hated the necessities of city life on those occasions; how I longed for a child-oriented culture.

Once on the bus Bobby was confronted by a wealth of possible activities. In New York buses there is one horizontal bar between the driver and the exit door and another facing the front, which was just the right height for Bobby to put his hands on and look ahead. There is also the fare box into which the money goes, with its fascinating click-click as the cash is automatically counted, and the small bar which the driver presses to release the fare coins from the position where they are visible down into the bowels of the counting machinery.

Bobby liked to stand at the front, holding the bar, looking ahead and then sidle up to the driver as near as he could get and press the coin release bar. Some of the drivers got to know him and allowed this to go on; I always made a point of saying a quick word of explanation and a thank you to these Bobby-tolerant drivers. There was one driver on the 86th Street crosstown bus who was so consistently considerate of Bobby and allowed him to be himself with such regularity that I regard his contribution as a sizeable one in the overall story of Bobby's entry into the outside world. I hope he reads this; I would like him to know what a valuable service he is giving to the sanity of the next generation.

When in a bus with a tolerant driver, I could follow Bobby's wishes and dissociate myself from him to a large extent. That gave me the opportunity to give some attention to the public. I would spot the disapprovers and give them a quick run-down on Bobby; I would also spot those with the light of curiosity, sympathy or even cooperation in their eye, and rapidly explain what it was all about.

Normally I would not talk about a child in his hearing or even in his presence if out of ear-shot. This rule was so rigidly applied in Toronto that we would not talk about one child if he or any other child was still in the building. Bobby was a special case: our excursions were so public and Bobby's need to make contact was so great that it was absolutely essential to enlist the public's support; so I broke the rule and talked endlessly with people about Bobby and the work. He mostly ignored me and never, to my memory, objected. Perhaps on a few occasions he told me to 'sit there and read your book'. In which case I, of course, sat there and read my book. Had he told me to stop talking to the public I would immediately have done so.

When Bobby started to play bus receptionist, it took me a little time to realize what he was doing. Needless to say, some of the people he 'received' never did realize what he was doing, in spite of my non-stop explanation.

He would stand at the front, close to the bar, pulling the entrants in and pushing the leavers out. Although the pulls and pushes were not heavy they were nonetheless noticeable

enough to startle those who received them. Sitting near the
entrance I could see their faces; most people registered surprise, sometimes surprise and anger. Either way, I would
rapidly give them a second surprise (people don't approach
strangers on New York buses) by giving them one of my
public-relation quickies, followed, if possible, by an
introduction to Bobby. But he would not accept an introduction or be friendly to a stranger who had been directly hostile
to him. I remember with sadness a woman sitting near the
entrance of a bus, who reacted to Bobby's enthusiastically
rapid entry with 'Watch where you're going!' as her toes
were nearly trodden on. I apologized to her for Bobby and
told her about him. She mellowed instantly and wanted to
become a friend and ally. I called Bobby, and started to say,
'Bobby, this is Jane, she is sorry she shouted at you.' But as
soon as he saw who he was to meet he turned and ran away
shouting, 'No! No!' Though Bobby would immediately for-
give Mimi, myself and other regular helpers for our human
lapses, forgiving a stranger was as yet in the future for him.

Although it is a principle of the Children's Hours method
not to try to understand what the child is thinking, it became
impossible not to see Bobby as playing the helpful receptionist during his bus-passenger receiving act. I do not believe
there is any question that, in his mind, he was helping people
to do their thing. In my experience it is natural for a child
that has been allowed reasonable freedom in the early days
to want to help other people do whatever they are doing. So I
believe that Bobby the receptionist was beginning on the
socialized behaviour he had missed out on at an earlier stage.

So long as Bobby confined his activities to the front door,
interventions were not necessary. The side exit, with its
double doors, was a different matter. To Bobby there was an
infinity of available learning experiences to be gained from
those doors. He would climb up on the railing by the side of
the exit steps and press the button labelled 'Push to open
doors'. Anxious passengers sometimes tried to stop him

climbing the railing; then, as he leaned from the railing over the steps to push the button, there would be mutterings of 'He'll fall!' or, worse still, 'He'll hurt himself!'

Oh, those words, 'You'll hurt yourself!' They will, I forecast, reverberate in my ears on my deathbed. Bobby did not hurt himself and was at no time in danger of hurting himself except when people intervened or threatened to intervene. I will affirm over and over again from my own observations that children do not hurt themselves, provided they can see all that the adult can see. Accidents are caused by adult intervention. Let me state here that during the nine months in my care, Bobby did no damage to himself or to any property, with two exceptions, one of which was a paper stapler, and who has ever seen a paper stapler that could stand up to a child?

I was always on the alert for anyone old, disabled or child-carrying. Bobby was for some reason slow in understanding disablement; he did not seem to grasp that you could not push a person who was using a stick. At about this time my hip was bad and as well as using a stick I had to tell him that I could not walk far. He was very curious and solicitous about my hip, but did not modify his actions for members of the public with sticks. Concern for the welfare of strangers was something he had yet to develop.

A report on Bobby's progress (by Mimi)
Whatever Bobby's conscious motives for his bus and subway activities, I was beginning to understand, both from talking to Rachel and from being with Bobby, that he was motivated from within by his own drive towards health. His activities were chosen instinctively; they were what he needed for his growth, and the more he could pursue them unimpeded, the more he was growing.

Linda stayed in New York until the end of June. On 20 June she wrote a report in note-form of the changes she had seen in Bobby during her time with us. Based on her notes and my records, here is how far he had progressed:

EYE-CONTACT: Although mechanical objects could always steal Bobby's glance and he still cut off completely if anyone called 'Bobby' with an implied order or request, he was now using his eyes to relate to people, particularly in one-to-one games. He would play a game with Linda in which he came up eye to eye with her when they met, smiling and saying 'Coo-coo' as a password between them. He continued to direct role-play, telling us to 'Make happy! Make sad! Make nervous!' in quick succession, looking throughout into the face of the person he was directing.

SMILING AND LAUGHTER: Bobby was producing a lot more smiles and laughs in the games he conducted – like 'Buggy', which he played with Lisa at the Green School; it was a tickling, pick-bugs-off-each-other game, full of screams of laughter.

Another game of pretence was with a sign next to a fire hose on the wall of Rachel's hallway. 'DANGER' said the sign in red letters. Bobby, who was beginning to know that some things that said 'DANGER' weren't dangerous, often requested to be picked up to touch the sign. Having touched it, he'd pull his hand away as if it had been burned. Alternatively, he would almost touch it, commanding, 'Say DANGER!' So we'd say 'DANGER!' and he'd jerk away. Or he would want one of us to touch it, and act out getting hurt. This game produced lots of laughs, though it was strenuous for the taker as the sign was rather high up on the wall.

These were relatively simple games. One day he was on a subway train with Linda. In the early days he would get off trains wherever he wished without a thought except to go where he wanted to go. By this time he had started warning us, 'Get off here!' or 'Change for No. 4 Express!' making sure we wouldn't lose him. On this occasion before each stop Bobby announced that he was getting off, and Linda kept making ready to go. Then, at each stop, Bobby just sat back and smiled.

BODILY MOVEMENT: Linda commented that when she looked at Bobby from behind he often looked as if he were pulling his shoulders stiffly up. And she noted: 'A characteristic movement for Bobby is a fluttering of his hands in front of him with his elbows close to his body. He does this while jumping or running or quick skipping, which indicates to me a certain nervous excitement. The amount of times Bobby has used this movement has lessened considerably over the period of one and a half months that I have been seeing him. His skip often now has long strides and loose, swinging, floppy arms. This relaxing from a tight constricting body-form to a looser, more open one has been happening gradually. On the swing Bobby loosens up, letting his body and legs and head swing from front to back, even closing his eyes and humming.'

In any game, if he was really frightened or screamed to stop we stopped immediately. We never said, 'Don't be a baby!'; we respected him and his fear. So he kept the ground he had gained and was able to go a bit further the next time.

EXPRESSING EMOTIONS: When angry, Bobby would hit people who placed limits on his (to him reasonable) actions. He once hit Linda when she prevented him from pressing a particular lift button; then he told the lift operator, 'I hit Linda!' The man immediately turned the slightly tense situation into a game; he said, 'No, I hit Linda. I'm sorry and I won't do it again.' Bobby stopped and stared at this turn-around, then grinned at the man. Linda was amazed, too; but intuitive people are found in the most unlikely places, and you don't need training in psychology to be friendly to an angry kid.

Bobby still had panic reactions now and again, and would sometimes get hysterical in the lobby when Louise came to take him home. But he was learning to cope with frustration – accepting, for example, that the door of a lift he wanted to ride was sometimes closed to him. Best of all, he was learning to express his feelings verbally. USE OF LANGUAGE: 'Go to Rachel's! Go to 14th Street! Go to Brighton Beach! Go to Brooklyn!' Bobby would plead in rapid succession; when our day had ended and he had to go home he'd want to go everywhere, anywhere else. Formerly he had had to screech and drag his feet; now, like toddlers who cry less once they can speak, he could express his wishes and run away symbolically in words.

His use of language was still rather clumsy, though, with personal pronouns still usually mixed up.

Linda heard the occasional full sentence, her breath held as Bobby slowly chose his words: 'That's Bobby's house on the blue side of the building.' She once told me, giggling, that he had asked her: 'Will you punch Billy for me?'

Best of all, though, be began to recap his own state of mind, saying 'I getting upset,' just as we used to say to him, 'I see you're getting very upset.' His being able to say it meant he was getting in touch with his own feelings, and cared enough about others to communicate them. And just being able to put his emotions into words calmed him down – his tantrums grew fewer as his speech emerged.

Complete sentences or not, Bobby's speech was coming right along, and was as beautiful to witness as his freer body and his more expansive face.

10 Bobby Regresses

Bobby and Billy at home (by Louise)
Before Rachel entered our lives I had read all kinds of different viewpoints on children like Bobby, and, although many of these were discouraging, I had never given up hope. I felt that he was very bright, and I wanted to help him in some way, but I didn't know what that way was. I didn't want his mind wasted, because I felt he was capable of a lot; I wanted him to get to a point where he could start to do things and become whatever he could become. I never felt he was doomed; I always assumed that there was an answer, that he could be helped to become a normal person. It made me very happy to see that start to happen.

Ever since the trip to Provincetown, we had been seeing changes in Bobby and Billy, some of them slow and subtle and some much more obvious. The most obvious and immediately welcome change, from our point of view, was toilet training. Billy was pretty well dry before we left, and after we got back so was Bobby. Robert and I removed the hooks from the bedroom and bathroom doors so they had easy access to the toilet, and the boys chose to use it. There was a lot of plastic left over from Provincetown and I put it on their beds at home as a precaution, but from then on there was only one bed-wetting incident, when one of them had a bad dream. Robert commented that that alone made it worth the expensive trip!

By the time we got back, too, other improvements were showing. Bobby was beginning to make eye-contact, and to use the first person about himself instead of the third, though it took him a while to get his pronouns right. Billy's speech had improved enormously, and when he started school at the end of April he fitted in happily right away. The first morning he went there he made a beeline for the project table and within sixty seconds of walking in he was glueing pieces on a coloured box as if he'd been there for years. He settled down well, and now that Bobby and he were leading their own separate lives they got along much better together. They did fight sometimes, of course, but there was usually a reason for it, whereas previously Bobby used to attack him without any provocation, or even, seemingly, any real aggression. Of course the fact that Bobby was off my hands for long hours and Billy was at school gave me some freedom which I hadn't had since their birth; I could go out all by myself and do things I couldn't do before – including going into stores I hadn't been able to go into with the boys!

When Bobby arrived home he was usually upset that his Hour had finished; he would have liked it to go on. But by the beginning of April he was no longer creating those terrible scenes when he had to leave Rachel. And he was much more manageable at home. He no longer needed to move around the whole time and get into every place he could get into, or slip out of the apartment at inappropriate times. He was able to slow down and become absorbed in things.

He never told me what went on in his Hours, and I never asked him or Billy. I understood that Hours were private, and that if they wanted to tell me something, they would. Billy sometimes talked about going round Rachel's room and playing cooking games, but it was hard to picture what was happening. Rachel talked about showing me an Hour, but I think in New York she had no other children to give Hours to, and she certainly had her hands full with our two.

Whatever was going on, I could see something good was coming out of it, and I felt a great trust in Rachel. I had put the boys in her hands and whatever she wanted to do, I felt she knew what she was doing.

Of course, some of the things she was doing were hard to take. My most embarrassing moments were when I sometimes had to travel on a bus with Rachel and Bobby, after meeting with her or on my way to pick up Billy from school. I found this very hard, because when we got on the bus people would see that he was my child, but that Rachel was in charge. Bobby would stand on seats or want to go up to the front and look at the fare box; people on buses aren't used to that. They would be looking at me and wondering why I didn't say anything, while Rachel would be talking to Bobby, unselfconsciously recapping what he did. Sometimes people raised objections, and Rachel would tell them he was perfectly fine, but they would keep looking at me, wondering why I wasn't doing something – and why was this older woman letting him do what he wanted? I often wished I wasn't there!

At home, too, I wasn't quite sure how I should act with Bobby, and whether Rachel wanted me to continue with her methods or not. I tried to, to some extent, but there was really no way I could do what Rachel and Mimi were doing. I had the other children to take care of, and things to do in the house, so I couldn't just stop what I was doing at a moment's notice and be 'with' him. It bothered me that I had to tell him that I couldn't stop and talk to him right now, or that no, he couldn't do that – which I knew was exactly the opposite of what he'd been told all day. In fact I think this was much less of a problem for Bobby, who expected me to behave like a mother at home.

Of course, I couldn't help being anxious when Bobby was riding the subways. I wasn't worried about him getting lost because I knew he knew the system, but I was afraid he might run into some peculiar people. Robert, who would not allow ten-year-old George to travel alone on the subway, somehow managed to cope with the situation of four-year-old Bobby doing it. He took the view that if a child has to have surgery to remove an appendix there's always a risk, and the parents are always worried; if Rachel, whom we both trusted, considered that travelling and adventuring around New York was a necessary part of treatment, then we should accept that in the same way. In fact, Bobby never got lost and never seems to have run into any unpleasantness – and I got completely used to his being brought home by the police! Sometimes he would slip away from me, too, when we were outside; if I had Billy and Abigail with me there was no way I could run after him. So I would have to go home and wait for the phone call from the police, and explain to them that I couldn't collect him myself because of leaving the baby and Billy.

Very often it would be the same officers as last time who brought him back. I could see them looking at me, wondering why I wasn't agitated and upset and greatly relieved to see my child again. I was so used to it happening that I always remained very calm.

And it was all worthwhile. Bobby was progressing; he was heading in a new direction, and becoming a livelier, more real person all round. He was getting to know people, and that included me. He still had his own mind and his own ways, but through that summer he and I began making real contact. He was talking much more; if he wanted me he would call me and tell me what he wanted instead of just taking hold of me to show me. He would look at me as a person he recognized, with a new warmth and communication. And although he didn't initiate demonstrations of affection himself, when I put him to bed he clearly liked the physical contact we had, and responded to it.

I knew that Bobby was getting closer to Mimi, but I never worried that she was taking him away from me. I felt she was helping him to become a responsive person, and I knew it was easier for him to relate to her first because she wasn't his mother, and second because she wasn't the same authority figure that I was. His getting close to Mimi enabled him eventually to get close to me.

One way in which both Bobby and Billy showed their recognition of me as their mother was that they began to play a game of 'being born'. I don't remember exactly when the game started, but it was probably in May or June. They both knew the facts of birth; before Abigail was born we had told them all about it and they liked to touch my stomach and babble to the baby inside, or walk around with their own stomachs sticking out!

Once they were able to communicate with me, they started this game, which they directed. At bedtime I would have to lie down with each one in turn lying between my legs. Then I had to push very hard, saying 'Oh, the baby's coming – it's come – it's here! Oh, what a beautiful baby; I'm so happy!' It made me recall how I felt when I actually had the babies; I *was* very happy and exhilarated at the moment of birth.

It was very important to the boys that I was happy with them, and that when each one was born he was the best possible baby I could have. I would have to use their names as though the newborn baby arrived complete with its full identity. 'Oh, this is Bobby, and I'm so *happy* it's Bobby! What a nice boy!' Then I would hug them and hold them close, looking at their fingers and toes, and they would be very, very happy that I was so pleased to see them.

This game went on for a long, long time, sometimes for several nights in a row. Going to bed became quite a lengthy process. It made us all feel very close.

Regression (by Rachel)

I didn't know about these birth games at the time, but on the morning when Mimi left for her holiday, I had a serious talk with Robert Senior. I had been working with Bobby for nearly four months now, which left only just over two months before my contract ended. Bobby was doing well, but I was worried that two more months was not going to be enough. I knew that it would be enormously beneficial for him if he could go into regression.

We had had several instances in Canada of a child going spontaneously into regression during an Hour; that is, going back to an earlier stage of its life and living through some unfulfilled need or some trauma. Reliving traumatic early experiences under safe conditions enables children, and adults, to free themselves from the psychological pain around them, and to do the growing that they were unable to do at the time.

Some analysts see regression as a child's way of reacting spontaneously to an obstacle and they use this as a therapeutic tool. It needs very careful handling; I am very concerned about the ethics of regression, and this is one of the reasons why, if it does occur during an Hour, I insist on maintaining complete non-evaluation and non-direction, with which you cannot go wrong.

There are many therapies around now, such as Primal Therapy, which induce the state deliberately, but I would never induce regression deliberately in a child, any more than I would deliberately bring about some of the painful situations which had in fact led to breakthroughs in Bobby. Yet I felt that regression was what he needed; to go back to the emotional stage at which he had got stuck, when his autism was triggered off. One of my assistants in Canada had had many regression incidents; she was a highly intuitive person whose empathy during Hour-taking was such that children with her often spontaneously regressed to baby behaviour in some form or other.

I discussed all this with Bobby's father. The dilemma was that either we would do the job properly and free Bobby (and I couldn't do this without more time and skilled, able-bodied help), or just hand him back a reasonably socialized child. The only other person I could have trusted to do the job as well as I would have liked was in Canada, and could not help. So either we extended the contract or left the job unfinished. It was Robert's choice; I told him that I would work for expenses only, but I wanted to extend the contracted-for six months to an indefinite period. I didn't want to do a patch job on Bobby; I wanted a whole Bobby.

Robert wanted a whole Bobby too. His problem was that he did not have enough money to extend the contract. It was difficult for me to accept this at first; the family seemed well off, with their upper-class New York apartment and lifestyle. Robert made it clear to me that although the perquisites of his job made it look as if he was very well off, finding any further cash was impossible. All the same, I felt angry and thwarted.

That same evening Mimi came to my apartment to say goodbye before leaving for her holiday. Bobby was with me. He began snuggling up to Mimi in a way I hadn't seen before, he slowly took off her shirt and snuggled against her breasts, looking up at her the whole time. Mimi looked at me, somewhat taken aback, but I indicated to her that it was all right. It was like any small child getting into its mother's bed for a morning cuddle.

In my journal I commented: 'Bobby seems telepathic! He knew that we had given Pa the choice and he'd decided that he was going to take the law into his own hands. So there he was, undressing Mimi, snuggling up to her body, baby-like, womb-like. And I thought, "This is it. There's no going back now." '

There was more to come.

Our friends at the Green School had a programme of holiday outings for their kids, and at the end of June they invited Bobby and me along to two of them: once to a beach by a lake, and once to the zoo. The first trip, three days after Mimi's departure, was full of incidents.

I had explained to all of the school children beforehand that Bobby had to have special treatment. I've never known children not to accept that a child has to have special treatment. I explained that he had missed his childhood and since he hadn't had his playtime at the ordinary time, he had to have it now. Children are not jealous if things are explained properly; they understand special needs.

When we arrived at the school beach, Bobby was very excited about it. It was an enormously safe place, full of rescue men – very American. I couldn't imagine an English beach like that. I toured the security and life-saving personnel and introduced them all to Bobby with my customary quick explanation and request for their cooperation. They were all very friendly, the response was magnificent, and I felt relaxed and secure enough to be able to let Bobby go where he wanted in safety.

When he had been out of my sight for some twenty minutes I started a leisurely search for him. Away in the distance in the parking lot I saw an open car door; it was too far for me to see exactly what was happening, but around it I sensed tension. I thought, 'Oh, that's Bobby.'

I was barefooted, in a swimsuit, and the tarmac burnt my feet, so it took me some time to get there. When I did, I found a car with both front doors open and two very perplexed people, a man and a woman, who asked, 'Is this your kid?'

And then I saw him, sitting low in the back seat with an expression of utter serenity and dignity.

I said, 'Oh, has Bobby found you? He usually tries to open unlocked doors.'

'We were about to drive away and he just got in.' They were terribly perplexed.

I thought quickly. I had to relieve the anxiety in the adult faces, establish good relations all round, and somehow get Bobby out of that car, all as quickly as possible.

I said, 'Oh, I see he has adopted you as his temporary parents; he has selected you to be his father and mother for ten minutes of his life. What is your name?'

'Helga.'

'And yours?'

'Fritz.' All somewhat reluctantly.

I said, 'Hi, Bobby, this is Helga and this is Fritz, and this is their car.' And then I quickly said to them, 'He hasn't had a childhood, he's having it now.' Which was my best quick selling point. They slowly melted, and began to understand the situation, but they had been all ready to be hostile at first, and were still very perplexed.

So I said, 'Perhaps Helga and Fritz need to go back to their house, Bobby. Do you need to go back to your house, Helga and Fritz?'

Eager nods and yeses from both.

Now came the crucial moment. I still wasn't sure if I could get Bobby out of that car without using force.

'Bobby, I'm very sorry, but I'm afraid Helga and Fritz need to get back to their house and they are sorry they can't take you with them today. So I think you'd better get out and stay here by the lake.'

And Bobby got out, as good as gold. I was amazed.

The other two got in and shut their doors.

Bobby said, 'Goodbye Fritz, goodbye Helga.' They went off smiling at the end.

'Oh, he's great, that kid,' I thought to myself. 'He really is great!'

Before lunch, Bobby went a little way into the water. He wanted to take all his clothes off; the other children had gone into the changing rooms, but not of course Bobby, that would have been too programmed for him. I suggested he keep his underpants on. He seemed genuinely puzzled about this. I think he was wondering if he could urinate in his pants in the water. I took a guess and said, 'It's OK to pee in the water with your pants on.' He seemed to hear, which was unusual for him. I knew that he did hear my communications, but he rarely acknowledged that he had.

I said, 'Would you like me to come in?' and he said 'No,' but after lunch he said, 'You come in.' So I went in with him. He said, 'You swim out there.' So I swam 'out there', where he directed. Then he said, 'Swim to the rope. Touch red thing on the rope. Touch the blue one. Touch the white one.

Come back.' And I did what he told me to, again and again.
He was delighted. I think this was the first time that I had
seen Bobby delighted at another person's actions.

While I swam, he was paddling in the shallow part with
the water just below his navel. I was a lot further out towards
the rope when quite suddenly and quite unexpectedly he
started to walk fast towards me.

The water was very safe, with life-guards all over the
place, and as Bobby came towards me he passed two women
playing a game. But it was becoming quite obvious that he
was walking straight out, out of his depth, towards me, not a
bit afraid, just coming towards me. He was beginning to get
water in his mouth and was spluttering and jerking his head
in an effort to keep walking. Still he walked on towards me
with security and determination, and apparently to certain
drowning unless someone intervened.

The two women saw he was in difficulties and one of them
started towards him. I was about the same distance from
Bobby and moving fast towards him, too. I said, 'It's OK,
he's with me, please leave him alone.'

At first the woman didn't stop but I repeated my
reassurances several times, and when she saw that I was
obviously going to reach him at exactly the same moment as
her, she stopped, and I thanked her.

Bobby and I met in the water. I put my arms out and
caught him and he immediately let go all control, and relaxed in my arms, turning over and taking his feet off the
bottom so that he was floating on his back. I was standing up
in the water with my arms under his arms, holding his head
and shoulders up and his feet were floating, and he was as
happy as Larry!

After a time he asked me to take him out to the rope, so I
said, 'I'll try,' and took him out as near to the rope as I could,
wishing I were a stronger swimmer. I said, 'I'm sorry, I can't
go any further.' He accepted this. But the important thing
was that he was floating in the water having asked me to hold

him up, he was safe and he knew he was. We weren't swimming in any orthodox fashion; he wasn't on his front, he was on his back and he was blissful. We stayed like that for a long time, and I knew it was right.

I think this was a real regression episode. Bobby had a very good sense of danger and no way would he walk into a recognizable hazard. Yet he just waded out into the water, out of his depth until he was with me and I caught him, the security just oozing out of him. It was beautiful. It was a straight leap back into the womb. I was unable to respond to it fully and experience the maternal emotions with him because of my own insecurity in the water. However, I remained accepting, non-interpretative and non-directional, while Bobby regressed himself.

When Bobby had had enough we joined up with Susan, one of the teachers, who was jumping the other children in the water. Bobby joined her and wanted to be jumped up and down too, and then he wanted me to do it with him, gently.

I saw then that he was getting quite cold, although it was very hot in the sun, so we got out of the water and collected his towel. He spread the towel out on the sand, lay down and curled up on it. Picking up this cue, I collected as many other towels, my own trousers and everything I could find. I put them all over him and tucked him up, snug as a baby in a womb. He looked up once or twice to see what was going on. One of the other children came up and put some sunburn lotion on her back. At first he wanted some on his; but he was covered up with all the towels, womb-like on the sand, and didn't want them taken off, so he dispensed with it.

At the end of that happy day, I wrote in my diary: 'After this afternoon in the sea and that covered-up episode on the sand, there's no going back. We've got to go on with Bobby. I don't care who pays for it, we're going on with it.'

11 Summer

Basements and lifts (by Rachel)
We had some bad brushes with security men; Bobby, in his
emergence, was making more impact on the outside world.
Although I was finding him much easier to handle, and
although we were getting more people on our side, there
were also more times when we came up against the power
that New York security guards were able to wield against us.

In New York in 1977 there were security guards and
locked doors everywhere. The reactions of the guards ran the
whole gamut of human behaviour. At one end of the scale
were reasonable beings who were polite and helpful and
somehow managed to wear their uniforms and truncheons as
though they were decorative attire. At the other were
brown-uniformed, strutting, truncheon-waving men.

To Bobby they were all the same: inanimate objects to be
treated as navigational hazards, whom he bounced off as
though they were metal doors or dustbin lids. He had no
ability, and no need, to relate to them as human beings.
Their one common feature which did affect him was that
their security eye-level generally focused above the adult
navel. This meant that Bobby, whose head was just below
this height, could often join a group of adults and enter a
building unspotted. He would make a bee-line for the lifts
and sometimes could spend as long as two happy hours
going up and down. He was utterly safe; he understood more
about lifts than I did. I knew he was safe, he knew he was
safe; but the security guards and some members of the public
thought otherwise.

Basements were a particularly happy hunting ground for Bobby because he could often get into a lift at basement level, eluding the guards. All those rambling basements were also wonderful play areas in themselves. Unfortunately he was not supposed to explore them on his own; sometimes I would let him, while I stayed in my flat, knowing he was quite safe; but also knowing that there were those who would have expected me, instead of sitting down calmly and waiting for him to come back, to be chasing him and finding out where he was, or telephoning the desk staff to tell them where I was in case someone phoned up to tell me where he was. But because those lifts and basements were heaven for a child like Bobby, I took this calculated risk.

There were several tricky incidents with him during Mimi's absence. One day we were in a café; everyone in that café had been nice to him, but the café owner was nasty to him, and I lost my temper. Bobby came up and sat on my lap and said, 'For real, for real, for real, Rachel!' As much as to say, 'Don't be angry with anyone in front of me!'

Some of our outings were beautiful. On 12 July I recorded:

Took him at my house from Mimi. Bobby's partings with Mimi are getting easier.

NEW: Took little horse on wheels – first toy he has played with in the street. Rode it well. When I said, 'not over the road, but on the sidewalk', he accepted it well. Was *very* public co-operative with his horse. On one occasion he was riding it where there were lots of people – he stuck to the side. The horse had a list to the right, so he kept hitting the right wall. He kicked himself away from it several times. Then he got the idea of starting off at a different angle so that he had a long run downhill before he circled back to the right wall – bright, is that kid!

Round about that time Bobby and I found a big building that for some reason we could get into; most apartment buildings were well defended by security guards. Bobby was everywhere, up the lift, down the lift; there were people there, but they didn't interfere and were very accepting. So I allowed myself to follow him at a distance. And then I completely lost him.

I came out of the building to look around, and could see no sign of him. But from somewhere I could hear the notes of a church organ being played by inexpert fingers. I followed the sound and found that it came from a great empty church, with Bobby enthroned at the organ. I was worried that someone there might object, so I looked for the parson. When I eventually found him, I explained to him what I was doing and hoped he didn't mind. He was very understanding and hospitable and appreciated what I was doing; he invited us to come again. Bobby did re-visit the church more than once, with Mimi.

That parson understood that a church organ can be a plaything, and that to a child a plaything is as important as a church organ to a congregation.

Mimi got back early in July, refreshed from her holiday, and resumed her Special Times with Bobby. Her records also include several references to 'nice security men' and 'nasty security men'. She also found that Bobby's emergence was not all plain sailing; more aware of himself as a person, he was beginning to test out his limits with both of us.

Playing Mimi up (by Mimi)
Bobby and I were quite close through that hot and humid New York summer. In public, though, he began to play me up, and some of the time we were adversaries. He was no longer the autistic kid aloof from people; on occasions he behaved 'naughtily', to test his limits with Rachel and me, just as my own daughter, now aged two, is going through a phase of deliberately trying out my limits. And I kept saying to myself, 'OK, so much and then *no more!*' and then there would be no more. I took to carrying him around a lot on

piggy-back – he liked it and we could cover ground that way instead of constant stop-start that was his on-foot behaviour.

Between Bobby's behaviour and the heat, I was finding the job a strain at times but I had grown too close to pull away.

And it wasn't all me giving and Bobby taking. He was helping me too, to be outrageous, to talk to strangers, to find out why we could or couldn't do something, instead of blindly accepting other people's rules. I was finding out what mattered, remembering being a kid and wanting to explore the world. In New York, where I had learned not to stand out and attract attention, I was now learning instead to trust my wits and my own feelings. I was on the alert all the time, and Bobby accepted it when I said, 'Sorry, I don't want to go in there; it's too dark and it makes me nervous.' Real reasons were always accepted, though 'sorry, I'm sick of riding this subway' didn't count as a real reason, unless I was truly at the end of my tether.

The thing I found most difficult was being with Bobby in the presence of disapproving groups. I wanted peace, and would get uptight when people would start muttering 'Why doesn't she control that brat?' or some such remark. I'd rather be in the street, where the passers-by passed by instead of hanging around.

On 8 July, when I went to pick Bobby up from Rachel's, he had already taken off exploring on his own. So I went into the bank next door to her apartment block to take care of some business until he showed up. As it happened, that's where Bobby was, moving quietly among the grown-ups and children there. I joined a long line where I stood, watching dust motes dance in shafts of light, and there Bobby spotted me. Immediately, he started pulling down the red velvet ropes that marked the waiting line, screaming and running around.

I stayed in line, perspiring with heat and frustration, trying to stay cool, thinking that perhaps by ignoring him I'd affect him somehow. It would have been useless to try to 'control' him unless I was willing to leave the line and the bank; as it was, I was powerless until I'd done my business. He came to me from time to time, so people knew I was 'his' grown-up, and I got comments from, 'He's a handful!' to 'Brat!' Finally I reached the head of the line, and did my transactions, then I descended on Bobby, who was in the middle of the bank yanking on the ropes again.

'Stay in the bank!' he yelped as I took him by the wrist. 'No more bank today,' I replied grimly, and led the way out.

I was so distraught that I held his hand as he protested all the way upstairs to Rachel's flat. I feared that if I didn't and he ran away or got into any more mischief, I'd clobber him.

Once we were inside Rachel's, she worked her magic on us both. Stepping across her threshold was the end of the bank incident. The tension melted from both of us.

I'd like to have left him there, but Rachel had business to do, and I had to take him home. On the way he was into every door and every building after we got off the bus. Before going in to his apartment we stopped off at the Green School where we had a good time with Susan and Lisa and two of the kids. Bobby started typing out street numbers in a pattern on Lisa's typewriter. After a while we went upstairs to the school playroom, where there was an easel set up with paints. Bobby had never played with paints there before, but he set to and of his own accord made a painting of a large number ten in red, with accompanying blobs of yellow and red.

Three days later, at two adjacent easels, he made two paintings of '10', big and bold as before, in red and blue. He didn't care about keeping this work or bringing it home; the doing was the important thing. I never found out the significance of '10', and he never did it again.

Earlier that day we had come across a large number '19' on the wall next to a lift. Bobby knew what it was, but he liked to be told things he already knew, just as he would ask a person their name just after being introduced to them. So he asked: 'What's that?'

Mimi:	Nineteen.
Bobby:	(turning his head upside down) What's that?
Mimi:	Nineteen.
Bobby:	Sixty-one!

Sometimes I colluded with the grown-up world against Bobby and Children's Hours. One day he had gone to his father's office in the morning and I went to meet him at noon. Bobby was fed up with control and wanted to be out of the office, away from Daddy, into the lift and in the street with me. Instead, we stayed around; Robert suggested we three lunch together, and the idea of having lunch with an articulate grown-up had much more appeal for me than lifts. So Bobby had to join me.

It really wasn't that much fun, after all. Bobby was ganged up on by us two grown-ups, wasn't fond of the Chinese food, and didn't like having to sit quiet and still. No one really relaxed. But I was surprised at the self-control Bobby demonstrated: he wasn't really happy at the restaurant, but he was able to be there, postponing his desires and acting like a social being. It showed how far we had come.

Disasters and breakthroughs (by Rachel)

In the middle of July Bobby had another breakthrough. On our way home one day he darted down some basement steps. I decided not to follow him down, and started to stroll up and down the pavement. To my surprise, he came back up and indicated to me quite clearly that I was to stand at the top of the steps and not leave them. 'Don't walk,' he said. He came back a few times to check that I was still standing there.

This was one of the occasions when I interpreted his action, though its full significance did not dawn on me until I was writing up the record of that day's events. My interpretation was that Bobby had graduated to the point where he realized that security guards were people and not things. He had wanted me to stay within calling distance in case he was confronted by one. Suddenly, Bobby was faced with hostile people: he had entered the realm of personal relationships not just with friends, but with enemies. His negative emotions were no longer locked securely within himself but had an object: the security guards who drove him away from the lifts had become persons.

It was to be some time before he could express this hostility in any effective way, but this was the start. Bobby had discovered that enemies were human beings. I know many adults who have not yet made that discovery. It was a great day for Bobby and a great day for me.

The next day was quite eventful, too. Bobby had asked to visit his brother's school, where they tolerated and even welcomed our somewhat unorthodox visits. We stayed there a while, both of us happily pursuing our separate interests.

Time ran on and we were still there when Louise came to collect Billy. I asked her if she wanted me to come back with her and both boys. She said 'Yes.' So we all started off down the street together, and soon both boys were happily holding one of Mom's hands each.

Suddenly, Bobby took off into a cinema with an escalator and a hostile security man. By the time I had extricated him, having failed to do any good PR with the security man, Louise and Billy had gone on ahead and were out of sight. Bobby panicked, and screamed. He cried repeatedly: 'Momma, where are you?' I gently said, 'She has gone this way.'

Immediately, 'She hasn't!' cried Bobby, running off in the opposite direction.

His panic and hysteria were great. What he clearly wanted was for me to go away and for him to go home alone. This he was quite capable of doing, even though it meant crossing four streets and Third Avenue, but I never allowed him to cross roads on his own and this was no time to start. The noise was such that individual members of the public started to stop and try to be helpful. One offered a sweet; I was quick enough to frustrate that one without being noticed by Bobby.

Then a young girl asked if she could do anything. I was just about to send her politely away when out of my mouth, unbidden, came: 'Yes, you can help. Yes, you really can. Take Bobby home. What's your name?'

'Karlyn.'

'Bobby, this is Karlyn. She says she can take you home.'

Bobby trotted up, stopped crying, took Karlyn's hand and started for home.

It was the perfect solution. Bobby wanted independence from me. I wanted to give him that independence, but had not been able to because of road-crossing.

For a short time, Karlyn joined our team.

Two days later, Bobby and I took the subway to Grand Central Station, where Bobby immediately lost himself in the crowd. I started off to look for him, and eventually met him in the company of a large man who told me he was an ex-policeman. He also told me he had found Bobby at the place where I had last been with him, crying 'Rachel! Where is Rachel?'

This was another breakthrough. Never before had Bobby, when lost, gone back to the place where we had lost each other.

About this time, however, I realized that although the police were always friendly and helpful, and although Bobby had never come to any harm on his solitary travels, there is a point beyond which one shouldn't push one's luck. I decided that from now on Bobby should not travel on the subway except in the company of a pair of legs younger than mine, whether Mimi's or those of another helper. It was psychologically bad for him to feel that he was under supervision but there are times when one must compromise.

The next day when we went into the subway he shot ahead and out of sight. But not onto the platform. He hid around a corner, waiting for me to catch up. He repeated this several times in the next few days, always either waiting for me or coming back to me.

This was another breakthrough. It was as if Bobby was saying, 'I am free and able to travel on my own, but I am choosing not to.'

By this time it was becoming clear to me that once my contract was over I would be unable to stay indefinitely in New York. Bobby's father had no further funds, and it looked as though I would have to abandon my apartment and return to England. Mimi, however, could continue to work with Bobby, being paid as a child minder. So I deliberately encouraged the attachment that was growing between Bobby and Mimi to minimize the wrench of parting with me when the time came.

'Teensy' (by Mimi)

Although Bobby was being difficult with me at times, he could also be very affectionate. For some weeks now he had been saying he lived at 'Mimi's house', not his own. Now in July he started saying his name was 'Bobby Schlachter', or giving me his surname. It embarrassed me that his mother and father were hearing it, and perhaps wondering if I were trying to take over their son. It was also alarming – I sometimes feared that he was taking me over and might indeed move in! I kept my reactions to myself, though, and just recapped him, repeating the names he wanted or writing them down if requested to. My reactions had no place in his fantasy. (Rachel says that every child will want to belong to you, as you pass through the stage of being the most important person in his life, whether you are teacher, therapist, nurse, neighbour, or Aunt Mary.)

At the time of Abigail's birth he had been given a baby doll, about four inches tall, with blue eyes and blonde hair, like his sister. In mid-July he was taking her to bed with him (along with his subway map) and having loving conversation with her, in which he spoke for her, saying things like, 'I love you, Daddy Bobby!' I didn't know about this at the time, but it seems that he decided a live person was a better thing to cuddle than a toy, and towards the end of July Bobby started a lot of cuddle-play with me. In Rachel's bed or mine, nowhere else, he'd want to get under the covers with me and kiss, hug and talk. He also invented a character that I had to play, a little girl called 'Teensy'.

The cuddling started after we had had a particularly good day together, both considerate of each other. While on the subway one day without him, I noticed a connection that made a new route from my apartment to Rachel's. I kept it in mind without mentioning it, the way one keeps a present for a friend until Christmas. On 22 July, which was the next time we went into the subway, I told Bobby there was a new route and asked if he wanted to try it.

Bobby looked at me quizzically, as if to say, 'What, she knows something I don't know about the subway?' or perhaps, 'You mean you are beginning to enjoy the subway too?'

He led me to a map and we traced out the direction – uptown until 161st Street, then change to the IND downtown to the West Side. On that line, the nearest station to Rachel's was three blocks away from her place. On the line we usually used, the station was right outside her door.

Of course we travelled the new route that day, and Bobby discovered treasures I had missed in my reconnaissance – plenty of escalators at one station, an outdoor platform at another.

Finally we emerged from underground and, to celebrate, bought Coke from a vendor conveniently on the corner, then walked on to Rachel's. When we got there, he decided we should play on the bed, in and out of the covers. He put me under the covers and climbed in himself and put an arm round me. Now and again he said something to me in a calm voice, and we played and laughed happily together.

Four days later when we went out we had something of a battle. He had been pulling bus cords, despite my admonition that it was annoying to the driver. In fact, I felt it was calculated to annoy me when he went on doing it, and I decided to remove him from the bus. My record goes on:

> Up to Rachel's. He walked in her room with his arms open wide to her, and got and gave a big hug. A bit later he got in the bed and told me to come in with him, which I did. Played with dark and light awhile, in and out of covers. I was lying on my back and then he wanted me to face him. My arms had been to myself but when I put an arm around him he snuggled right up to me. We kissed a little, he calling me 'Teensy' and wanting me to have a baby's voice.
>
> When he asked me if I wanted to go out, I said I was too teeny. He made a noise, on a rising scale, and said now I was grown-up. I made my voice grow older as I 'grew up'. At one point, going from Mimi to Teensy and back again, he stroked my head and said, 'Poor Mimi, poor Mimi, poor Mimi.'

I also noted in my record for that day: 'Earlier he asked me something and I said, "I don't know." He said, "Don't say 'Don't know'." This happens often, also when I say "Maybe." ' Rachel told me that the desire to have everything controllable and clear-cut was very typical of children like Bobby; uncertainties are difficult for them to tolerate. She thought this somewhat explained his obsession with the subway, which was a learnable, controllable and unchanging system.

There was more cuddling on 27 July. We had a marvellous time that day. Bobby was testing his limits with me, but in a playful way. When we talked about going to Rachel's, he started mimicking Rachel, and had me do the same. I was in a good mood, and I had enough money with me to do all kinds of things – that was the day we saw fifteen minutes of *Orca – The Killer Whale*.

The next day we played a game involving Bobby's new awareness of other people. This is my record of it:

Played on the sidewalk awhile. A new favourite is 'Watch out for the people'; when I am holding him or his hand, I have to pull him out of the way of an imaginary crowd of pedestrians, crying, 'Watch out,' 'Move over,' or 'Excuse me,' etc.

When Rachel came back we all ate hot dogs (he had six) and then she took him off for the rest of the day. Variation on this involves pulling him away from imaginary traffic. Accompanied by roars of laughter, but it never goes on for long. I saw him try to play it with two different people on the street, but they didn't catch on to the game.

Later in the day we played 'Watch out for people' again. Then a security man drove by in the little truck they use and Bobby ran after him and jumped on! The man stopped and I retrieved Bobby, with thanks to the man.

The next day, 29 July, I noted another conversation with 'Teensy', the little-girl character I had become:

Bobby: Hi, Teensy.
Mimi: Hi, Bobby.
Bobby: Want to go out?
Mimi: Yeah.
Bobby: Want to take a walk?
Mimi: I'm too little. Can you carry me? Or push me in the pushchair?
Bobby: (with a smile) I'll carry you.

Teensy made a further appearance on 1 August:

Walked out into a thunderstorm, with teeming rain. (His decision to get wet rather than stay indoors.) He rode on me piggy-back, so his front and my back were the only dry parts of us. I was singing some rousing hymn as I strode along and he clung contentedly with head on my shoulder. At Rachel's he sent her out for hot dogs. I started to dry off, changing out of my wet shirt. He told me to keep my shirt off, touched my breasts and gently poked in my nipples.

Bobby: Hurt?
Mimi: No, that doesn't hurt.

Then he told me to put a shirt on and to get into bed with him. Lots of laughs, and a conversation with 'Teensy'.

Apart from a small reappearance the following month, 'Teensy's' life was restricted to this short period in New York. I thought at the time that she was his baby sister, but perhaps I was also playing Momma, or myself, or a future lover. Or Teensy may have been Bobby himself as a baby, while he took the role of the mother/grown-up. I couldn't interpret, but I knew Teensy was important, fulfilling his need to cuddle and be cuddled, and also to take care of someone else, even in fantasy.

We plan another trip (by Rachel)
Bobby was growing in all kinds of ways: sometimes these included being deliberately uncooperative, trying Mimi and me out; often he showed a new sense of cooperation. He was learning some practical things, too. At the beginning of August I noted:

> NEW: He has concept of not getting out of train because I can't get out without paying again.
> NEW: On bus I talked to him, beckoning first, and told him to be careful not to go up front unless invited by the driver. He accepted. I said to the person next to me, 'A week ago I couldn't have got away with that.'

And Mimi's record for 2 August includes:

He's knowing time lately, especially digital clocks. Apparently whenever I'm a few minutes later than my proposed time of arrival, it's upsetting. He doesn't give me a hard time, but I think Louise bears the brunt. We went to a few stores, he testing all the way.

One incident was a 'new' for me: Bobby, ahead of me in a subway, had grasped the moving handbelt of an escalator with both hands from the outside; it was beginning to lift him off the ground and I had visions of him being carried up to the top and dropping off. This was one of those rare occasions when the adult could see a real danger which the child couldn't. I shouted to him, 'Will you wait for me, Bobby!' and he did; he jumped lightly down, and didn't try again. This incident is important because it was the only time during the whole of our nine months together when I thought Bobby might actually be in physical danger.

Since the end of June I had been racking my brains as to how to do the best for Bobby in the limited time that was left to us. He was progressing fast; I wanted him to progress faster. But the set-up in New York did not allow for the twenty-four-hour-a-day help I would have liked him to have.

I remembered a meeting with two women from the Free Children's Commune, and how impressed I had been by their philosophy of group mothering and communal living. I visualized the commune in the hills, away from the city restrictions: no traffic, no security guards, no hostile members of the public! There Bobby and Billy could have as much freedom as they wanted, without having to be constantly aware of public opinion.

It seemed to me that this was a possible way of making the most of my last month with Bobby. I told Robert and Louise that the Commune sounded an ideal place, and early in July I wrote off and asked if we could stay there for three or four weeks in August, explaining our particular situation with Bobby. This is the reply they sent:

The Free Children's Commune, Inc., California

18 July 1977

Hello, Rachel

We are turned on by your interest in coming here. We do have some reservations concerning the children, specifically, where will they be going after their month here. We are reluctant to clear a child of the symptoms of reaction to a brutalizing environment if it is to return to the same environment. We will accept any child here provided that before the parent, or surrogate, takes it back the parent spends a week here to integrate with the child's new social reality.

It is difficult to respond to your request of 'keeping overall responsibility of Bobby'. The concept itself is somewhat alien being as all relationships here are based on equality. We picked this environment to maximize non-direction and liberty, and it is so felicitous here that by the time a child is two years old it requires no supervision. Thus the issue of 'responsibility' for a child of four and a half is virtually moot, unless there is a question of violence.

We can pick you up at the airport or if driving you can be met locally and someone will drive you up. We look forward to seeing you.

When I read this I thought that the negative points they raised might present problems, but that we could handle them; and as they ended up by repeating their invitation, I thought they thought so too. And I would have Mimi as moral support, should I need it.

12 The Long Trek West

California, here we come! (by Mimi)
On 4 August we set off. At 6.15 a.m. Robert taxied with
Rachel, Bobby, Billy and me to the Port Authority Bus
Terminal in mid-Manhattan. The boys were highly excited.
They had been up since 4.30 and had hardly touched their
breakfast. Billy announced that we were 'going to California
on a special bus – it's on the other side of Central Park!'
Bobby put him right: 'No, no, no, it's other side of New
Jersey!' At the bus terminal he checked to see that the bus we
were boarding said 'Los Angeles' on the front. It did, and
thus reassured we loaded up. Among our luggage, Louise
had included a supply of small toys, and one of Rachel's two
suitcases filled with food. Rachel said to Robert, 'Not to
worry, lad! We'll get a lot done this month.' We loaded up,
waved goodbye, and were off.

After two hours we hit Philadelphia (the boys called it
Filthy-elphia), and got off the bus to explore the station and
give them new sights to see.

After some argument we agreed to be aware of the time-
table but not to adhere strictly to it, being flexible when there
were frequent outgoing buses and firmer when they were few
and far between.

From the start, we decided to keep one grown-up in charge
of each child. At that first stop Bobby established that he was
with me, so it fell to Rachel to be in charge of scheduling.

We travelled to Pittsburgh (Pittsburger to the boys) that
same day, and I dashed off a postcard to Robert and Louise.

Bobby and Billy were having a wonderful time. They had

liked City buses in New York, but Greyhounds, with their adjustable padded seats and toilet in the rear, were much better. When they got restless we'd get off at the next stop and spend some time running around.

Nevertheless, the system is not designed for children, and we ran into our share of drivers and passengers who had no patience with our more-than-averagely active, noisy boys. Direct orders fell on deaf ears, but we got cooperation by politely asking the boys for it instead of demanding it. For example: 'Bobby, it's night-time and some people are trying to sleep and would prefer it quiet on the bus', or 'Billy, this driver gets nervous if you stand on the seat, so please sit down,' sometimes repeated several times, our sympathy always with the boys. We tried not to have battles of wills, so were constantly making decisions about what was really important, and then gently enforcing more limits with lots of apology and explanation. They did take notice of such requests; Bobby was now able to cooperate with others, and Billy tended to do what Bobby did. But we didn't want to restrict them too much.

From Pittsburgh we travelled all night to Indianapolis, Indiana, arriving at sunrise.

A couple of hours' travel that day brought us to St. Louis, Missouri. As usual on arrival, I took out our wide red ribbon sashes and nametags and distributed them to the others; the bus station was immense and rather crowded and we lost sight of the kids from time to time, but it's much easier to spot a kid when he's wearing a red satin sash!

We slept on the bus again. The boys were small enough to curl up on a seat to sleep, with head or feet cradled in our laps, but for adults sleeping on a Greyhound is much harder, and we were beginning to feel it. We arrived in Tulsa, Oklahoma early in the morning of 6 August. It was a bright, dewy, cool morning and the town hadn't yet woken up. To us that meant we didn't have to deal with any people – no PR problems – so we had a calm, unselfconscious walk through empty streets.

We spent the greater part of the day missing each other and missing outgoing buses. Finally, about 5 p.m. there was a bus, and we were all there at the same time. We surged on to it as though it were Noah's Ark on the last day before the Flood.

The sort of exchange Rachel had with the ticket man at Tulsa was a typical bus entrance dialogue:

Ticket Man: (seeing Rachel alone and looking at her Adult + Child ticket) Where is the child?

Rachel: Well, at the moment he's off on his own but he will probably be here before the bus leaves.

Ticket Man: How old is the child?

Rachel: Four.

Ticket Man: (with astonished look) *Four*, and off on his *own?*

Rachel: Yes, he's a rather special child, we have to let him free. He usually is back in time.

Ticket Man: (still more bewildered) Here's your ticket – come back when you've got him.

(Rachel retreats sadly, saying goodbye to the choice of seats for which she has queued for so long. Mimi and Billy arrive at the barrier. The ticket man clips tickets and says nothing.)

Mimi: I am travelling with that lady and the child with her; if the child doesn't come back in time I'll have to ask you for these tickets back.

Ticket Man: Why can't you all four stick together?

Mimi: Because the other child can't wait a long time in a line, so we wait for him.

Ticket Man: (nearly at the end of his tether) I've clipped your ticket; get on that bus with your kid.

(About ten minutes pass.)

Rachel: (approaching ticket man) I'm sorry, my kid hasn't turned up; may I get on the bus and tell my friend she'll have to get off?

Ticket Man: (looking around for a colleague to whom he can give the 'She's nuts' sign) Go on, then.

(Rachel enters bus, calls Mimi and Billy and retreats with them to the barrier. The bus leaves. Seconds later, Bobby arrives.)

Mimi: Hi, Bobby.

Rachel: Hi, Bobby.

Bobby: Hi, Mimi. Hi, Rachel.

Ticket Man: And all they can say is 'Hi!'

Rachel: Bobby, I'm sorry, the bus has gone.

(Bobby screams, runs to the barrier, is blocked by ticket man, screams at the bus to come back, lies down on the floor.)

Rachel: Sorry, we had to let it go, Bobby. The other folk couldn't wait.

(Bobby accepts this; the tantrum is short-lived. Interval of a few hours. Rachel approaches the same ticket man, this time with Billy.)

Ticket Man: Where is your friend and the other child?

Rachel: She is looking for the other child.

Ticket Man: Well, they'd better come soon.

(Rachel and Billy get on the bus. Bobby is seen ducking below eye level and boarding a different bus.)

Mimi: (to ticket man) Excuse me, may I get on just to retrieve my kid? He got on this bus by mistake.

(Bobby is sitting quietly in a seat amid perplexed passengers.)

Mimi: Hi Bobby, this bus is going in the wrong direction. Our bus is the one over there.

Bobby: I want to stay on this bus.

Mimi: Sorry Bobby, I know you like this bus but we have to join Rachel and Billy on the other bus.

(Bobby acquiesces and starts to follow Mimi out. At the driver's seat he picks up the intercom microphone.)

Bobby: Attention! This is the wrong bus.

(Mimi and Bobby leave and get on the right bus just in time.)

Small wonder that we got tired!

Travelling through western Oklahoma we saw some lovely countryside: a winding river, rounded hills, trees on riverbanks, lit by the setting sun. Enjoying the scenery was a rare relaxation for me and I made the most of it. By this time, our fatigue was beginning to tell. We got little sleep at night and during the day our attention had to be on the children, both in the buses and out of them.

On 6–7 August we had travelled through the night and at dawn again arrived in a new town – Albuquerque, New Mexico (named 'Apple Cookie' by our two). This bus station was brand new, with carpeting on the floor, cushioned seats, even a shower in the ladies' room. Alas, there wasn't time to shower, so I splashed water at my face, popped in my contact lenses, and was off with Bobby.

We clambered around awhile and went back to the station for breakfast with Rachel and Billy. Then off again westward on the bus, through dry country into Arizona. The driver on this bus, ill-tempered and not friendly to kids, kept telling the boys to sit down and keep quiet. He got so nasty that we simply got off the bus at the next stop, Holbrook, Arizona, a small dusty town.

Holbrook had little to attract us or the boys and we sensed that it was not that hospitable to travellers. Rachel said later that it was the first time on our journey that she was really anxious. This small town seemed as isolated and dangerous as the Wild West of the movies, and we felt ludicrously vulnerable. Rachel tried her usual methods of finding friendly people: looking in the phone book for doctors, parsons or Quakers, but had no luck. We met the next bus going west and were glad to be on our way.

The bus was not crowded as we boarded, but there were no adjacent seats and we knew from experience that the ride was more peaceful if we each sat next to one of the boys. Rachel approached the people sitting on their own towards the rear of the bus, and asked if they would be so kind as to change seats. She was like the hostess at a party, drawing out names and a little information, and introducing new seat-mates to each other. Most people were willing to oblige, and may even have been glad that she broke the ice for them. At least she gave them something to talk about – a travelling therapy group composed of a talkative grey-haired English-woman, a dazed young American woman, and a pair of bouncy little boys.

We were luckier in our bus driver this time and travelled that day without further incident, until we arrived at Flagstaff, Arizona, in the early evening.

The bus station had a pool table which attracted both our boys, and Bobby would sometimes grab the balls off the table in the middle of a game. Some of the pool players were tolerant, others not, but it was hard to keep the boys away. Finally I bought a game on the table for Bobby and he had a great time rolling the balls into the pockets, until the last one disappeared into the machinery of the table, not to be retrieved. Bobby reacted by screaming and running around frantically. At that point I took him away, and we walked off steam outside.

We meet Joe (by Rachel)
Next day was 8 August, our fifth day on the Greyhounds. We bussed all day through desert country, with no station stops, just one stop at a lonely country store-cum-gas station for Coca-Cola for everyone. I had long ago given in to Bobby's desire for Coke, though I disapprove of it myself. I loved the desert; I was enthralled by the cactuses, branching against the skyline. When we crossed the state line into California, the type of cactus changed as if they knew they had to change at the border.

Something else changed, too: the driver turned his rear-view mirror round. Perhaps California law didn't require him to keep an eye on the passengers, or perhaps it was his own decision; whatever the reason, I couldn't believe my eyes. I fetched Mimi and said, 'Do you see what I see?' Travel-worn and weary, we looked at each other as if all war had ceased for ever and every child had access to full play sessions. No mirror, *no mirror*, NO MIRROR! People got out of their seats and talked to one another; at least one card game was going on; someone else had pop music playing on the radio. The boys got into the spirit too; with no driver shouting at them they had no reason to react by being extra noisy or fidgety. Their behaviour, at a superficial glance, could have passed as normal.

By the evening, however, Mimi and I had had enough. The boys were as alive and full of energy as all well children are; Bobby still had a mind bent on the non-stop exploration of as wide an environment as he could create for himself. All four of us had slept when we could, but for Mimi and me it was difficult.

How we looked forward to our journey's end, the community in the hills where we could relax among people who understood us.

Into the midst of this exhaustion dropped Joe.

Joe was a large, red-headed, friendly, unaccompanied male. He was sitting in the farthest back seat of our bus; the toilet is also at the back of the bus, so the back seat passenger sees almost everyone after a while. Mimi and I had both noticed him, and *en route* to the toilet I had met him and talked to him.

There was a point when Mimi and I, tired and dirty, were not really coping with our tired, dirty boys, who by now were both unhappy and difficult, suffering from our lack of attention. Suddenly a big man came up to the boys with a wet cloth and gently but firmly mopped their hot dirty faces. It was Joe. Bobby immediately became calm and Billy followed suit. Mimi and I, who at any other time might have resented such 'interference', both felt that a great kindness had been done to us.

For the rest of that journey, Joe slid into our routine, if that word has any aptness to our situation. Quietly he would move in and take charge of one or the other child; he was directive, yet the children loved him. He seemed to see our adult needs, and responded exactly to them, making possible the much needed breaks for 'Mimi with Mimi' and 'Rachel with Rachel'. One child would go to sleep in the seat next to him and he would quietly say, 'He is with me,' leaving just enough time for me to smile or voice my thanks before I sank into a happy oblivion.

From the start, I trusted Joe, and my trust turned out to be well placed. He was just helping because he was helpful; a beautiful and, alas, rare quality. I told him something about our present situation and our overall project. He gave us his address and told us he lived on the coast himself with room to spare for all of us, if we ever needed it. The facts were noted in my address book, and we thanked him for his offer with no real thought of taking it up. At Brackensville we parted company; Joe continued north to San Francisco, and we were almost at our destination.

13 The Commune in the Hills

We arrive at our destination

A postcard had instructed us to join our hostesses at a motel at Brackensville. We examined the card and wondered if we could sleep as usual either on the bus or at the bus station; our travelling money was getting low. We decided that it would be better for public relations if we joined them at the motel, a decision which cost us twenty dollars and a taxi.

We fell into the luxury of the motel beds, not really bothering about who slept where so long as we got some horizontal comfort. I would have cheerfully accepted four in a bed in exchange for stretched legs at night.

When morning came Bobby and I emerged to find the swimming pool occupied by our two young hostesses and eleven-year-old Butterfly, all of whom I had met in Los Angeles. We joined them; the meeting was cordial and friendly, and the atmosphere relaxed. Mimi and Billy joined us, and after breakfast we loaded into their two cars for the hour's ride up into the hills.

As we were about to get into the cars I said to our hostess, 'Which seats shall we have? Let me play it carefully,' and tuned in to both the boys to see what would be best for them.

One of the women turned to me and said, 'There's no need to plan it! Kids can sit anywhere.'

I was a little surprised at this, but did not allow it to worry me. We had arrived; after our long, fraught journey we had reached our destination, and were looking forward to three weeks of country freedom. In the end, I sat in one car with

191

Bobby, and Mimi and Billy went in the other, arriving there
first.

At the commune (by Mimi)
We drove for an hour, through a dry desert area over sandy
ground between dark green brush and trees, then winding
up and up a dirt track on the outside of the hill, into
pinewoods at the top. We crossed through a gate, and below
us in a hollow some small wooden houses came into view: the
Free Children's Commune. We drew up outside the main
cabin, the community's eating and meeting house, and got
out.

There were several adults standing around, naked and
beautifully tanned, one woman breast-feeding a baby. They
looked at us unsmiling without greeting us or replying to my
'Hello'. Strange, I thought, but I didn't then feel that their
silence was hostile.

Billy asked for my hand to go down the uneven steps to the
cabin and I gave it to him. Straight away, one of the men said
to me, 'You're hampering his development by giving your
hand.'

As the newly-arrived guest, I answered blandly, 'Well,
he's a city kid and I'm sure we can gradually wean him to
where he's on his own.'

The man told me I was making the kid dependent on me
for my own gratification. I countered that I hadn't offered
help, the kid had asked me for it. We argued back and forth,
neither of us giving in, and I began to recognize the rhetoric
of the pamphleteer.

Rachel and Bobby arrived soon after, and I came in for
criticism once again. I was collecting the red sashes and
name-tags to stow them in my bag when one of the little girls
asked me if she could wear a sash. I said, no, sorry, as I
wanted to put them away. She said, 'Just for a minute,' and I
agreed, just for a minute. This decision was greeted by a
chorus of 'Ohs' and protests from the group. In their view

there should be no qualified decisions; a decision must be a yes or a no, and they permitted no conning by kids, whom they called 'expert conners'. In this case they had a point: I agree that if you say 'No' to a child you should stick to it.

Bobby and I went to check out the buildings and surroundings while Rachel went off with Billy and the commune children. The settlement nestled in a hollow in the hill, sparsely surrounded by pinewoods and circled by the dirt road.

As we explored, I became aware from time to time of the sound of raised voices cutting through the peaceful air; Rachel was getting into heated conversations with several of the commune inhabitants. From what I could overhear, and from the sort of remarks that were directed at me, I began to form a picture of the commune's outlook on life. It was not what we had expected.

The women who met us at the motel had seemed normal enough; they had been dressed in simple Asian-style robes and had names like those adopted by the devotees of Eastern religions, but that was not out of the ordinary in California in 1977. What was unusual, and disconcerting, was the behaviour of the rest of the people here, which ranged from unresponsiveness to outright hostility. According to their philosophy, greetings, smiles, thankyous, and simple courtesies were part of the false veneer of civilization. As I talked to them, it became clear that they distrusted and constantly questioned all relationships. They didn't believe in partnerships or marriage. They had sex, but said it was Tantric sex, not erotic sex; one type unites, the other divides. Possessiveness, whether of a sexual partner or a child, was not allowed. To them the dependence felt by a child was the neurotic product of the mother, not a natural instinct in the child; they contended that what children wanted and needed was the company of their peers, from whom they would learn, uncontaminated by adult values. And there we were with our clashing philosophy: that the full attention of grown-ups was vitally important to a child's healthy growth!

Yet the commune kids seemed fine; Rachel and I couldn't understand it. Of course, we weren't there long enough to observe closely, and indeed grown-ups were discouraged from bothering the children at their play. Except for the infants, the children all played together, seemingly without aggression. They didn't whine for attention; they seemed content. If they were hungry they secured their own fruit from the communal supply. I don't know if anyone cooked meals. We drank tea and ate fruit there, but did not have a meal.

Through the day we relaxed our one-to-one policy because there were so few dangers, and because Bobby and Billy were not about to wander away among the boring trees. This was lucky, in a way, since our relationship with the boys was the focus of the adults' constant scrutiny and ridicule. For instance, when we were out somewhere it was our habit to call 'Hi!' to each other at intervals, whether near or far, and during our short stay at the commune we kept this up. At one point I was up the hill some distance from Bobby; he said, 'Hi, Mimi!' and I said 'Hi, Bobby!' And behind me a male voice echoed sarcastically, 'Hi, Mimi! Hi, Bobby!'

At any rate, we had arrived, and I was glad of that after five days on the road. And although the people were making me irritable and uncomfortable, I saw the beginnings of something good happening to our boys. Billy was already steadier on his feet, and was tentatively joining the group of kids in their play. Shortly before, Bobby, who still usually screamed in terror at the sight of a dog, had actually reached out to the commune's dog as if to pat it; 'Doggy won't bite me,' he told me.

I returned to the main house after my smoke to find Rachel at the door, rigid with anger. Not far away, Bobby was walking up and down a stone path, very much in his own world.

'We're leaving!' Rachel announced.

'Whatever has happened?' I asked, and we drew away

from the house to talk in peace. Butterfly, obviously concerned and trying to act as peacemaker, joined us as we paced up and down the dirt road.

Rachel was fuming over a number of things, and particularly over the treatment Bobby had received in my absence. Still wondering if she wasn't over-reacting, I listened to her story.

We leave the commune (by Rachel)

When we arrived I stayed close to Billy and we explored the buildings and the surroundings with the community children. They were a bunch of apparently well and happy kids, naked in a wild country environment; they took us and showed us around.

The children seemed sensible enough, but it was not long before I became the object of aggression from the adults. I had gone inside a building with Bobby, and was concentrating on him when I was approached by a tall naked man who asked me: 'Do you really think children are in any way concerned with what an adult thinks about them?'

I composed myself to be very polite before replying that I could not answer a philosophical question while I was 'with' a kid.

'What d'you mean – *with* a kid? That's a load of bullshit!'

I got out of the building as quickly as I could. Some of the others followed me, hurling insults at me and telling Bobby that he should take no notice of me as I was only looking after him for my own gratification.

The criticisms and rudenesses continued. At one point Bobby said 'Thank you' to something. He was immediately treated to an aggressive lecture by the surrounding adults on the fact that 'please' and 'thank you' were words that had no place in a sane society, and I was lectured at length on the iniquity of allowing these kids to use such words. I was very much alert on this issue because despite all the non-communication of their early childhood, Louise had somehow managed to teach the boys to use these socially acceptable words, which was an enormous help with their emerging relationships. I was not going to allow this achievement to be sabotaged.

In front of the lecturer I said to Bobby: 'They don't like "please" and "thank you" here, Bobby, but other places they do.'

In fact I did not feel that the 'please' and 'thank you' issue was as much of a threat as some of the other colony values. Both the boys were already having to adjust to two different sets of values, ours and those at home, which could be roughly classified as Bohemian and conventional living. 'Please' and 'thank you' had a place in both worlds. It was not so much the prohibition of the words that bothered me as the lack of tolerance towards the child as he was, and the hostility with which the prohibition was expressed.

Bobby's reaction to the hostility was dignified. In the usual way he might well have reacted by screaming, but he didn't. He ignored the speakers and their aggression completely; they might as well not have been there.

Early on in our explorations we came across a dog which began barking at us. Bobby, as Mimi says, had slowly been becoming less afraid of dogs. He clearly wanted to be friendly with this one, but was unable to take the plunge completely: he would take half a step towards it, and retreat half a step back, whimpering, and flapping his hands in anxiety.

I stood near him, repeating over and over again, 'It's OK, Bobby, he is only barking and he won't bite if you stay there, he doesn't want you to come closer.' I varied the actual words while maintaining the reassurance and bodily and verbal closeness.

One of the colony members who was watching asked me, 'How many times do you think it's necessary to repeat yourself? He heard you the first time.'

I decided to ignore the sarcasm and answer the question

quite seriously. 'I think a thousand would be about the number, but it doesn't go by count, it goes by a measure of as long as the child needs it. A thousand is a guess.'

I think that this remark was received with a spit though I cannot be sure if it was an actual spit.

The same woman was with me later when I was with Billy, who was distressed about something; I was giving him close attention, helping him over his crisis, when she began to mock his cries in a very cruel way. I told her that I didn't think that was a kind thing to do. She replied that she was not a kind person, and that she would be herself. She then gave me a long lecture to the effect that all real emotions should be expressed and not hidden. At intervals in the lecture on 'being oneself' she went on mimicking Billy in the same sarcastic way.

I think it was this incident that made me realize that we could not stay in that place. But there was worse to come.

Feeling hungry, I went into the main building, where there was a communal supply of fruit. There was a group of adults in there smoking something that smelt odd. As I helped myself to an orange, Bobby came in looking for Mimi; she had gone out to smoke a cigarette, and not at that moment seeing me, Bobby began to scream in panic.

Rather than reassuring him that Mimi would be back, the colony's tactic was to tell him that Mimi was gone, dead, and he would have to make it on his own. I could hardly believe my ears. 'You don't need a mother!' they went on. 'She only wanted you for her own sake!'

I quickly stepped in, removed Bobby, still screaming, from the cabin, and reassured him that Mimi would be back soon. He quickly calmed down, but I did not. As soon as Mimi appeared I told her that we must leave, and we went out on the road to discuss it, accompanied by little Butterfly, who was anxious that we were so upset.

I told Mimi what had happened. She seemed rather dubious, having had different experiences from mine, but she agreed to go along with my decision to quit, and went to collect the boys. I went back into the cabin and found our hostess, with whom I had got on well at our meeting in Los Angeles, and asked to see her alone. She told me that there was no privacy in the colony; anything I had to say to her I could say to any member of the group.

This upset me considerably; I put a high value on private one-to-one dialogue. However, I swallowed hard and told her that we could not stay; could they drive us down the mountain while it was still daylight? While we were still discussing this, Mimi came up to me and asked me to reconsider my decision. Despite the state I was in, I had to admire the way she did it.

She asked me to take another look at the resident children and notice how calm and secure they appeared to be. She also told me that Billy was steadier on his feet, and that Bobby had related well to one of the dogs.

I could not believe that the degree of hostility and sarcasm which had been directed towards myself and observed by our children would not rub off on the children in a damaging way. I also felt that underlying the colony children's apparent calm there might be a great deal of depression. 'It won't get better and could get a lot worse,' I said. 'We just can't fit in with these people; they are not interested in dialogue or in anyone else's philosophy. They just want to impose their own.'

Mimi agreed with me about that, and reluctantly accepted my decision. Plans were made for us to be driven back to Brackensville. There was a two-hour wait, which was uncomfortable. Angry as they had been at our presence, the grown-ups were angrier still that we wanted to leave.

We had been at the commune exactly five hours. As we were loading up to go, it was arranged that one of the men should drive the car to the top of the hill before giving over the wheel to one of the women, because he was the more experienced driver and the drive up the hill was difficult.

The woman driver and two other women who came with us kept up a non-stop barrage at me; how I wished I had had a tape recorder!

The content of the attack was based on their philosophy of motherhood, which was in fact a nearly total denial of the role of mother: any caring for the child was a mother's power trip, and as such should be controlled.

At one stage, when the abuse was particularly loud, Bobby, who had been carefully listening to it all in the front with Mimi, turned round to face me in the back seat.

'Rachel,' he said, 'are you a doctor?'

'Yes, Bobby, I am a doctor.'

This dialogue was repeated several times, each repetition arousing fresh bouts of hostility in the driver.

During the past week or so Bobby had several times turned to me and suddenly asked, 'Rachel, are you a doctor?' As we went down that perilous mountainside I saw a possible connection between his question and what was going on in the outside world. I was being 'put down' by the women in the car; they were telling me I was wrong and a nobody. Bobby, by asking this question now was telling me, and perhaps them too, that I was right, and a somebody.

We made it safely to the main road and back into the city of Brackensville, where we were dropped off at the motel we had started out from that morning.

After this chaotic and disappointing day, we decided to spend the nearly-last of our money and took a room for a further night at the motel. The management were very friendly and welcoming, which was a relief after our recent reception. I telephoned Robert Senior, and between us we decided that the best plan was for us to meet him in Los Angeles in about ten days' time, when he was due to go there on business.

Mimi and I now had only one desire: to be horizontal. We

postponed worrying about the fact that to all intents and purposes we were refugees, with ten days to fill in and very little money. Aware of nothing but our complete exhaustion, we somehow dropped into bed; two beds between the four of us, not bothering who slept with who.

14 *Refugees with Joe*

The journey to Seatown

The management of that motel were marvellous. Early next morning while we were still asleep Bobby got up and started wandering round, stark naked. They didn't object or interfere, but telephoned me a little later to tell me that he was asleep, still naked, on a sofa in reception, and would I collect him as people were beginning to arrive. 'I'd let him sleep,' the girl said, 'but people are starting to come in now.'

By my standards it was an incredibly luxurious hotel, with a swimming pool in the middle of a partly grassed, partly green-carpeted, space surrounded by the motel bedrooms which all appeared identical.

That night Mimi and I had a conference. We were very short of money, having expected to stay at the commune, and having paid for our stay in advance. We were also homeless.

The first person who came to mind was Joe, and we decided to contact him in the morning and take up his offer to stay with him. When he issued it, he can't have imagined we would be getting in touch so soon! But I had had the feeling that he meant it. This decision made, we conferred about how other people treat their children and how we treated Bobby and Billy. We tried to understand what our personal limitations were, and why we were more nearly at breaking point than could be accounted for by fatigue.

It will be clear that Mimi and I do not like the conditioning method of child rearing but, and this is a very big 'but', we are fallible humans, and right at that Brackensville moment we were exhausted fallible humans. We took stock of this and listed the items of the boys' behaviour that we found most unbearable to ourselves, and then those items which we thought most unbearable to the public. During this process we found ourselves warming towards Louise; she had succeeded in producing two little boys with clean noses, socially acceptable eating habits and a correct use of speech; this last was even beginning to show in Bobby. These factors contributed to them both being, at the level of physical appearance at least, socially acceptable to their fellow bus passengers.

We decided to introduce conditioning for just one act of unacceptable behaviour. It was a formidable decision to make, going as it did completely against our basic principles. An optimum solution would have been to stick to our principles of non-direction, non-evaluation and full attention, while taking appropriate steps to become unfatigued. With limited money and further Greyhounds to ride this was not possible, so a compromise was settled on.

Then came the choice of what piece of behaviour to condition. After running through everything we finally settled on screeching. Bobby had a particularly high-pitched, ear-hurting screech which he turned on when cross or disappointed or when Mimi wanted to be on her own, and Billy had of course learned this from him. We decided that life without screeching would be a great deal more tolerable both for ourselves and for the public, and we decided to set up a no-screeching programme first thing next day.

In the morning we put both our resolutions into action. Joe took our request for asylum in his stride, and arranged to meet us at San Francisco that evening and drive us from there to Seatown, where he lived.

Before we embarked on our next series of buses we told the boys that from now on there would be 'no screeching'. The next time Bobby or Billy did screech my response was to remove the child bodily from wherever he was and replace him on his seat, saying: 'No screeching, tell me what you want in a normal tone of voice,' and then to thank him profusely when he finally complied. Off the buses I would take the child's hand and firmly march him out of the public area where the screeching was taking place. On one occasion when Bobby screeched in a café I did just that: I said, 'No screeching,' and, holding his arm firmly, I marched him out of the café and walked him round the town while he protested loudly that he wanted some food. We passed several cafés which I would not let him enter so long as he continued to screech. During the whole time I had my attention firmly riveted on him, and as soon as he said, and I knew that he meant, 'I want to go in here and no screeching,' I let go of his hand, thanked him, and in we went and enjoyed a happy, non-screeching meal.

'No screeching' was one of our good projects. It became a game; the boys loved it, we loved it and the public loved it. The message was clear to the boys: screeching was annoying to Rachel, Mimi, driver and passengers; Rachel and Mimi would stop it by force if necessary. There was no mention of screeching being 'wrong' and it was understood that in different places with different people it might be allowable.

The public reacted to our boys and to us much better when their ears weren't assaulted by screams, and our trip to San Francisco was much more peaceful than our previous Greyhound travels.

We arrived late at night, cold after the journey through agricultural central California. The boys were slumbering and we carried them off the bus in sleeping bags, but they soon woke up and went exploring the bus stations: parked buses, pinball machines, doors in and doors out, playing the driver in empty buses.

Finally Joe arrived in a friend's van which he had borrowed complete with friend in order to meet us. They drove us to Joe's home in Seatown; it was a large trailer in a mobile home park. Mimi, Bobby and I shared a big double bed in one room, there was a single bed in another room for Billy, and Joe slept in the living room on a chair-cum-ottoman. As he was used to going to sleep in this while watching TV he was quite happy with the arrangement. Gratefully we moved in and relaxed.

Life at Seatown was bliss for Mimi and me from a physical point of view; we had comfortable, horizontal sleeping space, the boys had the freedom of no bus drivers' mirrors, and Joe had his too-large-home filled with grateful guests. It was one of those all too rare arrangements whereby all parties gain and none feel exploited. We relaxed and lived, and I tried, not always successfully, to forget that there was neither plan nor money for September.

The neighbourliness was village-like. We very soon found out who Joe's friends were; they welcomed us and invited the boys to join them for meals and expeditions. We also found out rapidly who Joe's enemies were; these tended to be the same people as those who were upset by Bobby's presence.

The section of the mobile home park that Joe lived in did not allow resident children. The first morning we were there Bobby got up and out before the rest of us, attracting the attention of a hostile female neighbour, who called the police. When they arrived they talked to me, and then took Mimi aside and asked who we all were and what we were up to; they had presumably already questioned Joe. Satisfied that at least we weren't kidnappers, and were visitors rather than residents, the police took no further interest in us.

The neighbour did, however. She, and one or two others, lost no opportunity to telephone us: 'Get your child out of my garden or I'll call the police!' 'Can't you control your child?' 'If I catch him I'll give him something to remember!' As always, Bobby did no damage and did nothing that was dangerous, but he provoked in those who complained of his conduct a fear of the unfamiliar, coupled with an expectation of behaviour similar to that which they had experienced from other, so-called normal children.

That first day we spent most of our remaining money stocking up with food, and exploring the place. Seatown was a small seaside settlement with rows of bungalows alongside small roads, and a few shops a long walk away. Between Joe's trailer and the sea there was a hill, a large, sandy dune with footpaths running all over it among low bushes.

The only black spot for me in Seatown, apart from the spiteful neighbours, was that the sea air and open space of that hill were marred by the paths being used by under-age motor-cycle riders, revving their engines, falling off, braking in a way that caused the cycle to rear like a horse and occasionally tip over onto its rider, and other highly entertaining antics forbidden and inappropriate on USA highroads. To me, the noise of these machines breaking the peace of the country hurt; it hurt my adult ears. But to Bobby these motor-cycle antics were a joy. In fact they were the only good thing to be found on what to him were hateful life-and-subway-distant dunes.

Resourceful as ever, he found many mechanical things to explore, even in the dunes on the way to the sea. One of these joys was a tractor-cum-bulldozer that was being used to mend a gate which was sealing off a stretch of beach against motor traffic. Bobby 'assisted' in the process while Billy stayed well out of the way and I worked hard at the job of getting the workmen to accept Bobby as a mature mechanical mind housed in a four-and-a-half-year-old body. On this occasion I succeeded well, and Bobby made good friends with the workmen. By the time the operation was over both the tractor driver and his assistant were behaving as though they were in the presence of someone very special. They were. People who have the courage, as Bobby has, to be themselves and resist society's indoctrination, are very special.

I still look back on those days in Seatown as a happy

respite for all of us, not least because of Joe's acceptance of us. Although he did not really understand what we were doing, Joe was consistently kind and considerate towards us. He was a warm, good, generous, helpful person; I am grateful to him.

At Seatown (by Mimi)
During those days, both boys continued to take advantage of their freedom to go on growing. Now Rachel, surprisingly, tried something new.

Our treatment of Bobby and Billy was always to follow their lead, rarely suggesting activities to them. But at Joe's place Rachel got the idea, the feeling, that our boys were ready for some directive play material; that is, the grown-up supplies something to play with, with the expectation that the child will accept it. She produced, apparently from nowhere, some large watercolour brushes and a pot of water and gave them to the boys who were on Joe's concrete patio outside. Both of them started happily 'painting' with water on the concrete, and on the side of the trailer.

This was indeed an innovation. When we first met Bobby he had to be self-directive in every activity, to the extent of being 'deaf' to all suggestions and questions. He wouldn't think of doing something someone else wanted him to do. Billy, in imitation, also ignored much communication. Now they could accept a plaything from a grown-up and give it a try-out. Rachel and I left them to their fun and quietly rejoiced over this new stage in their growth.

That day Bobby had a mild stomach upset; he seemed to be over it next day, but the following night, when I was putting him to bed, I was trying to lull him asleep, my hand on his stomach to soothe him. At the same time my mind was already in the living room, wanting to join in the conversation with the other grown-ups. Bobby must have sensed my frustration and double attention, because he looked at me comically, and neatly and knowingly reversed our roles of adult and child. 'Mimi relax,' he said. 'Relax' was my usual instruction to him!

During this period, too, Bobby's attitude to Rachel began to change. For some time now he had not only been very possessive of me, but had been going through a phase of rejecting Rachel, at least when I was there. At Joe's he began to accept her more, and did not always want me at his side. On 16 August, after five days at Seatown, he allowed me to give Billy a piggy-back and himself crossed a street separately with Rachel. In the afternoon, when we called Robert Senior on the telephone, Bobby sat on her lap while he talked to his father, something he hadn't done in my presence lately. And at supper he chose to sit next to Rachel instead of me. Rachel later commented that it is usual for people, when rejected by a child who yesterday was friendly with them, to feel rejected and behave accordingly: 'Aren't you going to give me a kiss today?' The child, however, must be free to reject; we call it 'reject love', knowing that the child, while rejecting you, still loves you.

During that afternoon phone call, Robert confirmed the date of his business trip to California and he and Rachel worked out a scheme by which we would all stay together in Los Angeles.

One morning, while I was getting up, Bobby wanted my attention and I didn't feel like dealing with him or any of his requests. Not being Rachel, I told him to go away. He showed me what he thought of that cold answer later on, by instructing me, as 'Bobby', to say 'Hi'. I said 'Hi, Mimi,' to which he replied. 'Go away!' What a slap in the face.

We had done simple role-play before with the game of 'Make happy, make sad', but getting us to reverse our roles was something new. We were to play other roles in the weeks to come, acting out other painful scenes, all at Bobby's request. He intuitively saw the value of role-reversal, that if we can briefly be the other person we can understand them better. And that if a scene can be played back, it can be examined. Rachel often quotes an old Red Indian saying to the effect that you should never criticize a man until you've walked a mile in his moccasins.

Bobby and Billy spent that afternoon, our last in Seatown, with a neighbour, Sue, and her son, Zane, who were from the 'kids allowed' section of the trailer park. The boys behaved beautifully, she reported, though she had known what she might expect from them. They had all eaten together and later gone shopping, driving around in their van with no bizarre behaviour. Not long before, Bobby would have been incapable of staying with a group for any length of time; he would have had to take off on his own. I saw this as a breakthrough for him.

Early on the morning of the 19th we all packed into a neighbour's van and took the highway from Seatown to the Greyhound station at San Francisco. Bobby and Billy asked us a hundred times for information and reassurance. 'Where are we going?' 'Where are we going tomorrow?' 'Where do we get off?' This had been their litany ever since we left New York, their questions coming thicker and faster the more our plans changed. That day they were continuous.

But we were all in high humour; the nomads glad to be going on the road again and Joe glad to be getting his quiet home back. He gave us a final helping hand with our baggage at the station, kissed us goodbye and went off lightly down the street.

We caught a southbound bus almost immediately and left San Francisco. The boys were seasoned travellers by now, and we would be meeting Daddy at the end of the journey. It was a peaceful day on the Greyhound. At one point I wanted to take a nap, away from our crew; there was an empty seat in the middle of the bus, to which Rachel suggested I repair. She stayed with the two boys in the far back seat, the only one for three people, and kept talking to them.

There was no screeching, no beseeching Mimi to come back. I had my nap, and this was the first time Bobby let me go peacefully.

15 Reunion with Father

At the Marina Pacific Hotel (by Mimi)
It was a relief, after all our travelling, to get to Los Angeles that evening, to be met by a friendly person at the Greyhound station (we were an hour and a half late), and to be chauffeured in comfort to our new place to live. As with Louise in Provincetown, Rachel foresaw a problem of dual authority, since we would be living at close quarters with Robert, but Robert seemed quite happy at the prospect of a fortnight with us, and unperturbed about our change of plans.

We drove through Los Angeles downtown with its neon lights, turning onto the freeway after a while. The Marina Pacific turned out to be a modest, respectable seaside hotel, a short walk from the beach, with a sandy children's playground in between – ideal for normal family holidays.

As far as Bobby was concerned the most important feature of the hotel was that it had two lifts! His eyes gleamed. When we arrived on our floor, he insisted on taking the key to open our door, fiddling with the lock for several minutes before he gained entry. Robert had taken an apartment for us, with a living room, kitchen, bath and a bedroom whose bed, king-sized, could have slept four; he had already taken the adjoining room with bath for his centre. Billy chose to spend the night with Daddy, while Bobby slept in between Rachel and me in the other room.

That evening and over the next few days we filled Robert in on the details of our trip and the abbreviated visit to the commune. He was relieved that we hadn't stayed; he had been making some inquiries about the place, and after our departure from New York had received some disturbing reports about it. In fact, believing we were going to stay, he'd been planning to drive there from L.A. and check it out for himself. He was very pleased that we were all safe and sound under one roof.

The next morning Robert and Billy went out together to play on the beach; Rachel gave Robert instructions as to how a kid should be 'handed over' from one adult to another – the adult in control must act decisively, she said, with no butting in from other adults. The other three of us went to visit Rachel's friend, the mother of Bruce, the child to whom Rachel had given Hours during her previous visits. She had been longing to see Bobby and Bruce together, as they were both exceptionally bright and both unconventionally behaved. Bruce was about a year older than Bobby, and they didn't exactly click; they fought the afternoon away, instead. They didn't feel the kinship that Rachel had hoped they would, but finally they seemed to call some kind of truce and left each other to play alone.

Bobby was intrigued by a motorcycle parked outside; he looked at it, climbed on it, and made motor noises. Later on in the day the owner, a friend of Bruce's mother, took each boy for a ride on it. Bobby was overjoyed at the prospect and nearly orgasmic on the ride itself: I saw them come around the corner towards home, and Bobby looked like he was trying not to let his joy spill out all over. When he got off he was very calm and dreamy.

The next day Robert took Bobby out with him; they strolled around the locality, watched the Venice body-building team, and spent a long time in the playground. Robert observed that Bobby was making a good effort to distinguish his behaviour with his father from his behaviour with Rachel.

Our first few days in Los Angeles were spent in and around the hotel, on city buses, at the Greyhound station, at

Daddy's office and in the homes of friends of Rachel's. Most of the time I was with Bobby, at his insistence, and sometimes we'd grate on each other, especially when indoors or confined somehow. My biggest ploy to get him calmed down was to take him for a walk on the beach, or carry him piggy-back if he didn't want to walk. I'd have him on my back and start running across the sand towards the surf. Getting near was fun, but getting in it was terrifying. Bobby didn't like the surf at all, didn't want to get in the water or dodge the waves, but the sand was okay.

We took some long walks and explored lifeguard stations – locked when the lifeguards left for the day but still with windows to look through.

By our third day, after a couple of visits to the Greyhound bus depot studying the local maps, Bobby had completely mastered the local bus system! So, after starting his morning in his usual way with nude ramblings on the lifts, he took off and rode buses by himself. We weren't worried that he'd get lost; we knew by now that he wouldn't, and he was, as always, clearly labelled. When he came back, however, he was in the company of some giant, black-shirted Los Angeles policemen, who immediately started to attack Rachel and Robert: 'Is this your kid? What d'you think you're doing?' Bobby, who had always been friendly with policemen, was screaming hysterically. Rachel and Robert laid on their professional cool and tried to explain what we were doing. The policemen didn't want to know, and Bobby was clearly scared.

We never got the story of why he was so upset; perhaps the cops were unfriendly; perhaps in his characteristic reaction to brusque authority he had made them mad.

The same day we also found ourselves in trouble with the hotel manager, who told Rachel that we had to go! Bobby was inconveniencing the other guests by 'possessing' the lifts by pressing the call button and, when the doors opened, controlling their shutting with his hands. Rachel wrote in

her diary: 'His motivation is clear; he needs to check out the
control of the shutting both by the automatic mechanism
and by his own power.' However, Bobby was somehow
shuttling between the two lifts, one at each end of the corridor, so that both of them were tied up – and even Rachel
had to admit that his activities were anti-social as far as the
other guests were concerned.

But she PR'd the manager so successfully that he became
an ally. He told Rachel and Robert that he admired what
they were trying to do and would cooperate fully with us,
within his responsibility to the rest of the hotel.

Mimi is driving (by Rachel)
Next day we went out on a picnic. Bruce had come to stay
with us for two nights, and the party consisted of the woman
in the apartment next to ours, her two children and her baby,
Bruce, Mimi, myself and the two boys. Mimi was driving
Robert's hired car. On the return journey there was a long
talk about Bobby's choice of where to sit: in front on my lap,
or in the rear seat. He had great difficulty in accepting the
issue of a choice. Eventually he settled for being behind
Mimi with everyone except myself and Bruce, who sat in the
front. Bobby stood behind Mimi's seat almost touching her
and talking to her; she was still the unrivalled number one in
his life.

Suddenly, Bobby leaned forward, annoyed about something, and hit Mimi smartly over the head. Mimi braked
sharply, swerved, and shouted at him. Instantaneously I
dived over to the back of the car, grabbing Bobby firmly by
the hair as I dived. I landed in the back head first with my
legs in the air and my fist still attached to Bobby's hair. As I
performed these undignified acrobatics I said, firmly but
without anger, 'Mimi is driving; Mimi is driving; the driver
has to be left alone to drive. You can't stand near her. Mimi
is driving!'

I was sorry that the visiting mother, who had only had a

day or two of seeing our methods, was present to observe such apparent violence. It is important to stress that the violence was only apparent; at no time was I angry or even appeared angry with Bobby, or conveyed to him that he was naughty to hit Mimi. When I had got my legs disentangled, no mean task for a sixty-eight-year-old with a bad hip, I released my grip on Bobby's hair and held him firmly on my lap.

Bobby was screaming, 'I want to be with Mimi, I don't want to be with Rachel!' Simultaneously I kept repeating, 'Mimi is driving and Bobby is with Rachel; no screaming, Mimi is driving,' and periodically Mimi joined in with 'I'm sorry, Bobby, I'm driving; I will be with you when I'm not driving.'

Eventually we reached home, all very tense. Mimi was shaken by the near-accident; Bobby was angry at the indignity of being restrained; and I was feeling awful about having had to use force instead of finding some way of avoiding the situation, particularly in front of our neighbour, who had only just been introduced to the concept of Children's Hours. Mimi quickly took Bobby off, and I lay down on the couch.

A little later Mimi came in, almost at the end of her tether and near tears. She said, 'It's awful; when he hits me I feel like hitting him back.'

We had a long talk about this. There are times when hitting back is the correct thing to do, and I told Mimi so, but it has to be turned into a game. If a child who loves me hits me, I receive the hit as love, telling him so, and I repay the hit exactly, and with love. If the child gives me a hit that hurts I will say 'That one hurt,' and then I will give him one of exactly the same strength. I must emphasize that the hit is reciprocal, not retaliatory. There is never any anger or malice in the reciprocal hit, and it is important that the adult should keep his own emotions out of the game; any real anger immediately destroys the effectiveness of the method. When hitting is treated as a loving game, the child who has started with an aggressive hit on a place that hurts ends up by giving a love-pat on my eyelid. This is a very effective technique but it has to be played just right.

Mimi and I began to feel better as we worked things out and went on to help each other over the difficulties of the difference between force, which can be necessary, and violence, which never is. I was still lying on the couch with Mimi sitting on the coffee-table beside it, when Bobby came in. Seeing us there together, a delighted glint came into his eyes. Suddenly he ordered Mimi: 'Drive the car!'

Mimi, not knowing what he had in mind, started to pantomime driving. Bobby looked at me, then went up behind Mimi and started to choke her. I took my cue and dragged him away from her, saying, 'You can't do that, Mimi is driving!'

Bobby was laughing!

Then he said, 'I'm driving,' and started to turn the imaginary wheel. He cast us in different roles: I had to be Bobby and had to cry; in fact he gave me a specific order to cry harder. Then Mimi had to drive again and Bobby was Rachel. As Rachel, he told Mimi to stop the car and love Bobby, played by me. As the game continued Billy came in and joined us; we all changed roles with every possible permutation, and played them with gusto. Bobby's screams were larger than life; Rachel's somersault was turned into an acrobatic feat and Mimi's shock and recovery were enacted with vigour. By the end we were all yelling, laughing and having a thoroughly good time, as we did on the next day, and for several days after that when we played 'Mimi is driving' again.

It was a wonderful breakthrough on Bobby's part. He had never heard of the word 'psychodrama' and theory played no part in his activities. But rather than internalizing his bad feelings he had instinctively found a way to bring them out in the open, look at them, play with them, and command the anger and pain to appear and then disappear. Children often play out painful scenes with dolls; Bobby played this one out with the people involved, and we were all healed by it.

More games (by Mimi)
Bobby used play both for his own growth and just for fun. There was one game I had played with the two boys on our long bus trip by folding my thumb into my fist to make a 'mouth' and giving each hand a name and a personality. Ralph and Lefty were the original ones; Ralph was sort of like me and Lefty was a sneaky backbiter. Later they were joined by two more personalities, Teensy, the baby from New York, and Smoky, a deep-voiced drawler. The boys would clamour for one or the other, have them talk to each other, have them come and go, and they occupied us happily for hours.

The 'What's your name?' game developed out of Bobby's habit of asking us, and other friends, 'What's your name?' in the same way that he'd ask 'What's that?' about something he already knew: a bus, a lift, a toy. He liked to hear the names spoken, and several times a day we'd find ourselves saying, 'I'm Mimi', 'I'm Rachel', 'That's a car'. Rachel told me that this is normal behaviour in two-year-olds when they're learning to talk, which Bobby was still doing.

There came a time eventually when we began to play with the answers, giving someone else's name or a false one. We always took note of Bobby's cues and reactions, and knew whether he wanted to hear the sweet sound of our names or was ready to play with the concept. Rachel told him that she was Jemima Jehosophat Jehenkinson, to his great delight. And I resurrected for myself Philomena Hassenpfeffer – actually a name my mother used to use in similar games when I was a child.

In Los Angeles, Bobby began to join in the game in a new way.

Bobby: (calmly) What's your name?
Mimi: Mimi.
Bobby: (patiently) What's your name?
Mimi: My name is Mimi.
Bobby: No! What's your name?
Mimi: Philomena Hassenpfeffer.
Bobby: (smiles)
Mimi: What's your name?
(Slowly, for the first time, Bobby forms a play name for himself.)
Bobby: (with great seriousness and dignity) Feeny Heiker Hoker Tem.

We didn't actually use the names; Bobby was never Feeny except in the What's Your Name Game, the only place where I was Philomena or Rachel Jemima. But it was beautiful to hear him come out with it. The next day he told me a new name for Billy as well: 'Ha Por Hed'.

Bruce was with us for a second night, and in the evening all three boys had fun taking a bath together. Off his own territory and outnumbered two to one, Bruce was aggressive to Bobby; in fact the two of them at one point collaborated in a game which really would have got us evicted if the hotel management had heard about it. Our fourth-floor apartment had a balcony directly above a small café attached to the hotel. Having discovered that they could bombard the café with pencils, Bruce and Bobby experimented by peeing from the balcony. Fortunately they didn't allow for the wind, and their ammunition hit the pavement instead.

The next day, the already crowded apartment became more so when Robert's eldest son, George, joined us for the rest of our stay. George's mother, Robert's first wife, was able to get cheap flights for him through her work, and he often joined Robert on his business travels. George, like any normal ten-year-old, adopted what he thought was grown-up behaviour by trying to keep Bobby in line by force, and he took a dim view of our 'freedom' therapy. Luckily, he got on well with Billy, who was more easily kept in line and saw George as less of an interloper, whereas Bobby's status as oldest kid was usurped by his arrival.

We had some toys with us which we'd brought on the trip: dominoes, little cars, various stuffed animals. The day of George's arrival, Bobby built the first thing I ever saw him make: out of dominoes he made an enclosure for two little Volkswagens, a sort of garage, with separate stalls for each car. The building was entirely closed with no doorway. Rachel, although normally advocating non-interpretation, nevertheless on this occasion took me aside and interpreted the two cars as Bobby and Billy, and the closed garage as their world, walled in. Bobby came back to it later, swung open one wall, drove one car out, and closed the garage up again. If we are still interpreting, though we don't convey it, which brother was the car that drove away? Was it Bobby, setting himself free from his enclosed world?

The next few days continued much as before, with the addition of George to our number. There were visits to Daddy's office, and to the playground where Bobby one day buckled one of his own shoes for the first time, there was the beach and there were the buses, buses, buses. . . . Bobby and I spent one afternoon going over a couple of maps of the USA and California, tracing our routes, noting every stop we'd made, the places we'd stayed at, the names of the people we'd met. In the evening Rachel, Billy, Bobby and I played again the game of 'Mimi is driving', letting off a lot of steam in the process.

Our second week in Los Angeles (by Rachel)
I was finding life in L.A. somewhat tense. I knew that I must talk to Robert about continuing our programme with the boys, and I was putting it off. We were now three adults and three boys, living at close quarters; all of us with different needs and different attitudes to life. But I could see that good

things were happening with both boys. Billy was developing much more freedom and independence. One day he strayed further than usual on the beach and was brought back by a lifeguard. A day or two later, he went off to the nearby playground by himself; he came back and then returned, still on his own.

Bobby continued to be more accepting of me in Mimi's absence and presence.

We were due to leave the hotel on 1 September, when I planned to stay on in L.A. for two weeks' holiday and the rest of the party would return to New York. Sunday, Monday and Tuesday of that second week, I noted as 'a most eventful continuous breakthrough three days for Bobby'.

On the Sunday the two boys, Mimi and myself visited some friends of Robert's who had a swimming pool where Bobby spent a long time with Mimi, lying on an inflated floater in a womb-like trance. He was seeing nothing in the outside world, he was totally absorbed in his experience. It was a fantastic sight, a beautiful womb drama with Mimi.

This is an interpretation of course, but the picture came over completely clearly. The blue-and-white floater on which Bobby was lying was the womb; Mimi was holding onto it, treading water, so that the floater was an extension of Mimi-as-mother; Mimi was away, too, absorbed in just being there looking after him; and I was there, also, giving moral support to Mimi with my presence. I could see that it was going on a little too long for Bobby's physical well-being; he looked cold and, tuned in to him as I was, I knew that he was hungry. It was important not to bring him out too suddenly. I swam up to the floater where he lay entranced, with his eyes closed, and said very casually and naturally, with absolutely no demands in my voice, 'Hi, chaps, time for out!' I swam away, Bobby opened his eyes in his own time, and when he was ready Mimi pushed him to the side.

On the next day, Monday, it was decided that Mimi

would take Billy and George to Daddy's office, and that I would take Bobby. To my surprise he accepted this quite calmly; he made an affectionate advance towards me, and we went off on the yellow buses. Later on, we visited an alteration tailor who had some chairs for waiting customers; I sat down, while Bobby lay on the floor sucking a bottle top, apparently in continued baby play. This tailor was an understanding man, and did not interfere.

Two days later I had an excellent report from Mimi and Robert; Bobby had joined the other two boys on a visit to Robert's office. He was introduced to the office staff, with whom he was a great hit, and stayed with adults rather than taking off in search of machinery. At one point he did start getting bored and screechy; Robert told him it would only be a little while longer, and Bobby at once settled down to wait patiently. Shortly after that Mimi drove him back to the hotel, a little nervous lest he jump on her while driving, but as there were just two of them he had no need to demand her attention in that way, and did not do so.

Later on they went back to pick Daddy up, only to find that something had come up at the office so that Robert could not leave at the time planned. As they drove away with George but no Daddy there were huge screams of 'Daddy come back!' So Mimi had rather a harrowing drive, though Bobby still felt no need to jump on the driver. He had had a big let-down and protested at it fiercely, but was then able to assimilate and accept it.

We were to leave on Thursday; on Tuesday Robert and I discussed the future. I wanted to go on with Bobby's treatment; I made various suggestions as to how we could manage it on a smaller budget, but Robert could not afford to go on. Bobby and Billy were no longer the unmanageable little boys they had been six months before; Bobby was able to communicate, to play, to wait, to show affection to the father to whom he had been 'deaf'. Billy was more able to be himself instead of his brother's reflection. And Robert appreciated what we had done. But he could see no way of continuing the contract.

At about this stage Robert commented that Bobby still had certain characteristics that were not 'normal'; his habit of running up and down and flapping his arms still continued, though to nothing like the extent of six months before. He also still had a low tolerance of frustration, and his speech patterns, though enormously improved, were individual, to say the least. He seemed to invent his own grammar, constructing questions for instance in a binary way: 'Gimbels is open Gimbels is closed,' meaning, 'Is Gimbels open or closed?' 'What grey letters is?' was Bobby's way of saying, 'How do you spell "grey"?'

There certainly had been progress, but I felt I was getting out before the job was finished. The family left for New York where Mimi would be helped by Fran, who was already familiar with my methods. Later I made my own leisurely way back to New York and it sadly began to come home to me that my time with Bobby must soon come to an end.

16 Weaning

Second return to New York (by Mimi)
On 5 September I was supposed to hand Bobby over to Fran. In fact I was ill that day, so she had him on her own, and seemed to have coped very well. She was a student in Special Education, a calm and competent woman in her early twenties, short and stocky with dark frizzy hair. She was with us for most of September, taking Bobby during my two weeks off and then either taking Billy or joining Bobby and me as a foursome.

On 7 September I returned to New York and Fran was on her own. From her records she seems to have understood Rachel's methods and carried them out well from the start. Early on, she recorded a small gem of Bobby behaviour, on 9 September:

> Bobby decided to walk his father to work. He held his father's hand the whole way (at least half an hour) and Robert remarked that it was the longest continuous hand-holding they had ever had.

Perhaps our stay in Los Angeles had enabled father and son to come closer together.

Meanwhile, Bobby was becoming more and more possessive of his mother; he always wanted her to be home when he got back from an outing. On 9 September Fran noted:

> He went home willingly, but when he got there Mom wasn't home. Doreen and Billy were. He didn't want to go in the house until she came home. He cried and threw himself on the floor. After some coaxing he finally went in.

Later in the month, 20 September, my own record includes:

> We got to Bobby's door, Bobby saying Momma wasn't home, 'Is Momma home?' etc. (She was planning to go out that night.) She was still home. He punishes her when she goes out. She is not sure how to act.

These double emotions went on as long as I knew Bobby – he didn't want to go home, but when he did get there he wanted Louise to be there too. He was getting closer to his mother all the time. Although Rachel's methods are carried out independently of parents, they don't have the effect of separating the child from his parents, and Bobby's relationship with both parents definitely improved during the time he spent with us.

With Fran, Bobby added toy stores to his repertoire; this was a new interest, as with one or two exceptions toy stores hadn't attracted either of the boys before. They continued to be an attraction after my return. In various combinations of Bobby and me, Bobby and Fran, Billy and Fran or all four of us, we visited several stores, especially F.A.O. Schwartz, New York's famous huge toy emporium on Fifth Avenue.

On 19 September I came back on duty and had to work my way back into the schedule after a quiet two weeks off. Bobby and Fran came to my home for lunch that day. In my eagerness to see him, I came out of the apartment onto the stairs, instead of giving Bobby the pleasure of knocking and being received; he made it clear that that is what he would have preferred by covering his eyes at the sight of me!

Covering his eyes seemed to be a new way Bobby had found of coping with something he didn't want to face, rather than relying on his old habit of screeching and running away. He did it once or twice during the next few weeks. Once was on 26 September, when Fran and I delivered him to his block and told him we wouldn't be seeing him for two days. Bobby's response was to close his eyes in a comic-melodramatic way. But then he opened them and repeated calmly to Fran, 'Tomorrow you take Billy. Wednesday we'll see you.' It was astounding that he could accept the disappointment like that. As luck would have it, the kid who lived across the hall from Bobby came in at that moment and the two of them went upstairs together. Bobby could leave us, who had disappointed him, and be sociable with someone else.

On this first occasion, as soon as he was inside my apartment he came into my arms, grinning, and then became absorbed in examining the innovations to the place since his last visit, in particular the puppy. 'Doggy bite you?' he inquired, but without anxiety. Then he took me onto my bed for some hugs, telling Fran to 'Go away!' from the bedroom door while we cuddled.

The next day Billy joined Bobby, Fran and me for an outing which included another visit to F.A.O. Schwartz. I was impressed by how happy and well-behaved he was – I had heard from Doreen and Louise that he had been 'fresh and mouthy' since coming back from L.A., but we didn't find him so. Maybe he acted differently with us, or perhaps we acted differently with him; I was by now so used to recapping the boys rather than reacting, for instance saying calmly, 'I see. You think I'm a silly old cow,' rather than 'What a naughty thing to say!' which would egg them on to further 'naughty' remarks. Children say and do antisocial things to get a rise out of grown-ups; ignoring them is no good, but on the other hand reacting in a horrified manner is no good either. Both encourage them to continue. Our calm recap let the boys know they were heard, and that we still accepted them as people, so they could go beyond grown-up-baiting into the next stage of growth.

On 22 September, during our travels, Bobby discovered the uptown station at 125th Street. From there you can go downtown to Grand Central Station, or north out of the city altogether. On that day I hadn't enough money even to go to Grand Central, but we returned four days later with cash in hand, and got on board. At Grand Central we watched trains, rode in lifts and on escalators, and had a Coke. And an Amtrak engineer let Bobby play with a few dials and buttons in an engine. Then when the man tried to prevent a few actions, his co-worker said: 'He wouldn't be a natural boy if he didn't try everything!'

Little did that man know that calling Bobby 'a natural boy' was music to my ears!

And something good to tell Rachel, who had returned to New York that week.

When Rachel arrived back in New York she continued seeing Bobby, giving both him and Billy Hours, but also weaning them both from totally attentive methods, treating them more as friends, so that separation, when it came, would not be too traumatic. Among other things, Bobby became an occasional house guest in her flat.

On 4 October, Bobby stayed overnight with Rachel for the first time. When Billy and I arrived there we ate hot dogs and played around, until I was getting tired and ready to go. Bobby, however, wasn't interested in leaving. Rachel was willing to keep him with her, and he to let me go, so I left.

Later in the evening Rachel called me to say he was still with her. Bobby got on the phone and we talked for an hour. He conversed lucidly, and told me he lived in two houses – at his own and at Rachel's. Then he asked his usual questions about where I lived, where did certain subways and buses go, followed by his affectionate 'poo' noises over the phone. I enjoyed myself thoroughly during this unusually flowing conversation. Eventually, I initiated the end, saying I would talk five more minutes, and he then said goodbye.

That night was Bobby's first of several overnight visits, mostly at Rachel's place and once at mine. She saw these sleeping visits as a great step forward in Bobby's growth.

The first time he stayed at my place was on 20 October, after he'd spent another night at Rachel's – altogether he was away from home from Wednesday morning to Friday evening!

Rachel wrote to Louise about his visits:

> I'd like you to realize that this is a major breakthrough and I didn't expect it so soon . . . From now on his independence will thrive and it will be great for his growth (I don't like the word 'therapy') if he can stay in as many houses as possible – of course always at his own request. He must never (except in very dire emergency) be made to do it.
>
> He is progressing at a great rate and this is all part of it. On Monday Mimi and I visited the kids who have been left to drift (at an autistic unit) – it was horrible.

And this is Rachel's record of his third visit, on 19–20 October:

> The most striking thing about Bobby staying is how very undemanding he is. When he asks to stay in the evening (four-ish) and I say 'Yes', Mimi goes and he plays by himself, sometimes talking to himself, nearly always about subway maps, and occasionally coming over to give me a hug.
>
> This is in striking contrast to other lone kids who are always demanding attention. It may be because of his basic autism, or it may be because he is so saturated with full attention after eight months of it that he can afford to be not demanding.
>
> As I write this in the morning he has put a little pressure on me to come out, and when I said not before nine he accepted it gracefully, with a little opposition, but very little.

At the end of October Bobby and I had the most beautiful walk with my dog. It was towards sundown and we walked leisurely through Central Park, throwing fallen leaves, running and shouting, watching joggers silhouetted against the sky on the reservoir path. Bobby left us several times to look at the joggers more closely, then came back to walk on – dogs were not allowed on the runners' path. It was one of those precious moments. The weather was fine, the setting beautiful, and all three of us, the child, the dog and myself, were in harmony. We had come a long way from that first day when I had carried a screaming, screeching stranger across the Park.

Separation begins (by Rachel)
By New York State law, Bobby was required to start school at six. Nearly all American parents, however, start their children in kindergarten at five, and in October Bobby, now five, was eligible for kindergarten, paid for by the state. The American legal system is such that every child has to be educated, and if there is not a suitable school within the system the authorities will pay the fees for a private school. We all realized that Bobby was not yet ready for an ordinary school, and probably not even the special education department of an ordinary school, but he had a right to go to a school for children with learning disabilities. Even then, he would first have to go through bureaucratic processing by the New York City Board of Education; this was set up for November. Meanwhile, his parents and I went hunting for possible schools.

In the process of hunting I acquired a thick card index of the places we saw, including schools, autistic units, and another unit with autistics in it. The more we looked the lower my heart sank. I saw nothing that could offer Bobby anything.

One of the places we visited was a hospital where there was an autistic centre and programme. It had been recommended to me as a good place. It was awful. The inmates were older and taller than Bobby, and after behaviour modification were able to do simple things like tooth cleaning. When a bell rang they lined up for whatever the next thing was, and just stood there, waiting. I went up and talked to one of them; then I asked one of the people in charge if it was all right to do so. He said: 'Well, you can, but we don't really like it.' I had a good chat with a lad about the fact that in England elevators are called lifts. But otherwise the children seemed like automata. Bobby was not going to enter a place like that if I could help it. We kept on looking; eventually a suitable school was found.

During this final period I often gave Bobby full days of attention, including outings. Louise supplied us with expenses and beautifully-packed sandwiches. On one such occasion, Bobby and I had both succeeded in getting through the door of the block opposite to the one he lived in. We got through unobserved whilst other people were going in and out, and had a legitimate excuse for being there, which was by no means always the case. The real reason was that Bobby wanted to go there; to ride the lifts, look out of the corridor windows and generally do anything he felt like doing. On this occasion we had rung the bell of two apartments where we knew the people; they were both out. Bobby had gone into a room labelled 'Janitor's Closet'. He was inside with the door closed; I opened it to see if he was still there, and saw a big, low wash basin. I apologized for disturbing him and waited outside till he had finished whatever he was doing. Bobby never did any harm to anything he understood, and there was nothing in that room that Bobby did not understand.

Suddenly, while he was still behind the door, the lift opened and a security man emerged, truncheon in hand, followed by another and another and another. Being sixty-eight, my mind instantly travelled backwards: five brown-uniformed truncheon-carrying security guards, closing in on me, with Bobby out of sight behind a closed door . . . visions of Nazis and cellar beating-up centres rose to my mind.

At that moment Bobby emerged, trying to pull his pants up; his clothes were chosen for looks rather than easy functioning. All five guards turned their attention to him.

'And there he is,' said one guard, approaching Bobby.

'He is with me,' I said, hastily moving protectively towards the child.

'He has no right to be in this building.'

'We are calling on friends,' I said, relieved that we had actually rung two bells of two real acquaintances.

One of the guards tried to talk to Bobby, who had backed against the wall, pants still only half up.

'Please leave him to me,' I begged, attempting to do up those complicated trousers. For one terrible moment I wondered if he had defaecated in the Janitor's room, but a quick look assured me that all was well.

I ended our confrontation eventually by saying we would leave, but please would they let me go along with Bobby in one lift, while they followed in another. They agreed, and I, relieved, went ahead, having at last secured those trousers.

When Bobby moved towards his own block, I said 'Cheerio, Bobby, see you tomorrow,' and waved him good-bye. One of his first acts of independence had been to go up in the lift to his apartment alone; an independence both he and I valued. But today one of the guards shouted: 'There you are, you see, you are letting him go up alone. Go with him. He was found in the drier the other day – he will get hurt.' I knew, too, that they were thinking: 'And we will get an insurance claim against us.'

Pursuing a policy of appeasement, I opened the door and called to Bobby: 'Sorry, lad, these men want me to go with you up to your apartment today. I'm very sorry, but I'm afraid I will have to come with you.'

Bobby protested violently, but I repeated my apologies and insisted on accompanying him.

This campaign against Bobby's independence, which was not based only on concern for his welfare, was unnecessary. He did not have one accident during the nine months he was with us. His sense of danger was superb and his knowledge of machinery as good as could be with his limited experience. I would happily leave Bobby alone in any of the situations he knew: trains, buses, lifts, escalators, streets and garages, if it were not for *people*. It was people, sometimes genuinely wanting to help, that were the danger.

I braced myself after this incident for a final concerted organized harassment from the total security force, about thirty men, who policed the four buildings. It did not happen; I do not know why. Perhaps even the establishment thought that five security guards were a bit excessive to gang up on one lame old lady and one five-year-old boy.

Meanwhile I was putting into action my decision to 'wean' Bobby. After his overnight stay with me, I had just been writing about how undemanding he was, when he suddenly became very demanding. It was almost as though he knew what I was writing, which at some level he probably did.

I put it to him that I couldn't give him an Hour on Thursday morning, but he could come downtown with me on my business, a visit to an official building, or go home. He completely understood. Six months before he would not have been able to comprehend the communication. He chose to come with me, but he played me up all the way, and we had worse lift trouble than usual at the building itself. The officials there were not nice to Bobby at all, and I was now acting as an 'ordinary person' as opposed to an Hour-giver.

It was becoming clear to me that I would soon have to leave New York. I could see that I was never going to get my work going there and there was nothing definite happening in Los Angeles for me until the following spring.

Very slowly, I came to the conclusion that it would be best for me to go back to England. I continued to see as much as I could of Bobby and Billy, and to give demonstration Hours to anyone who was interested. During these demonstrations I was also looking out for someone to take a special interest in the boys after I had gone.

Bobby and the outside world (by Mimi)

Bobby was continuing to relate happily to the outside world, making new friends and extending the boundaries of his exploring – although the outside world was not always so happy about him. Strangers still could not understand what Rachel and I were up to, and why we gave him so much freedom, and many people, sadly, were afraid to be at all responsible for him.

A couple of weeks later we found ourselves in a trying situation. Bobby and I were in a hot dog shop at the end of the day. We'd been in crowded stores and crowded trains all day and were ready for a break. He finished his hot dog, as I sprawled on a stool, and went off looking round the shop. He discovered a little door and unlatched it – at which point the man behind the counter roared: 'Get away from there! Get out of here!'

The man went on screaming and a couple of his friends joined in, all of them acting like Bobby was the slimiest criminal of the century. The little door led to some rather steep stairs, but they were only stairs.

'Come on Bobby,' I said loudly, 'some people are very rude!' Rachel later commented that for me to be able to say this in public was a real breakthrough. Bobby always knew I was on his side, but I was usually too shy to speak out. Out on the street I was still raving in anger at that crazy hot-dog man, but Bobby simply patted me and said, 'It's all right, Mimi,' a couple of times, until finally I had to laugh.

One day around this time, Bobby and I walked out onto a wet, snowy street after having some very satisfactory rides in the lift in Macy's department store. Outside, a Salvation Army band was playing Christmas music, with a woman singing into a microphone. Her song ended as we approached, and Bobby walked up to her. She was evidently used to small children's attraction to her microphone, for she passed it easily to him.

Bobby paused for a moment, and the woman suggested

that he say 'Merry Christmas'. Even as she was speaking, Bobby launched into an announcement that there would be 'Cash and prizes', gesturing dramatically like a game show host! The woman gaped, and recovered herself and her microphone, and Bobby left the scene unperturbed. I was giggling to myself, but not to Bobby. He had simply done what came naturally, with no sense of incongruity. We bent into the wind and continued down the street.

A friendship and a rebirth (by Rachel)
At last, in November, Bobby found himself a new friend to replace me. Esther was the organizer of the Westside Tenants' Association; an efficient young woman who worked by day as a research photographer. She was in no way a therapist, although she did child-minding in her spare time. I told her about my work with Bobby, and she asked if she could come along to observe an Hour, which she did on 19 November.

She and Bobby immediately became friends, and I was quickly relegated to second place.

When Esther telephoned me afterwards to discuss the meeting with Bobby, she said: 'If I hadn't known his history, I would have thought he was just an ordinary kid.' I phoned Robert immediately and said, 'Stand by for a special news bulletin – listen to the quote of the year!' and repeated Esther's comment.

During the first part of that session Bobby had been subdued; I had never seen him so subdued and was anxious and sad about the loss of his usual exuberance. But as soon as we went out he took off his coat and handed it to Esther to carry. Immediately he seemed much happier, and I realized that the restriction of his arms in his winter coat, while we stayed indoors, had been having a constricting effect on his emotions. I need to be reminded occasionally that moods can be of physical origin.

At the end of our outing we went back to Esther's apartment, and Bobby went in with her, shutting me outside! Perhaps he was preparing himself for the time when I would no longer be there. He stayed with Esther a long time, periodically coming out to check that I was all right. When it was time to go home, he wanted her to come too; unfortunately she couldn't.

After that Esther began to give Bobby Hours on her own, following his usual pattern of lift play, visits to Gimbel's, where she noted that he played with toys but didn't ask for them, and back to her flat where he played with her kitten, Meatball. She remained in Bobby's life for a long time after that, taking him out on Saturdays and being a very good friend to him.

Robert Senior was noting the changes in Bobby. Although his speech was still idiosyncratic and it was still common for him to run up and down, flapping his arms, he was now able to read, sounding out any words he didn't know; he could add and subtract; his memory was phenomenal, and he could remember many telephone numbers and addresses, as well as the complete New York City bus and subway systems! He could also remember the dates on which events occurred; when Robert referred to his flight back from Los Angeles with Billy, Bobby said: 'You mean Friday September two?' Robert checked it up, and it was correct. Bobby was also demonstrating real affection and concern for the important people in his life, including his parents.

Two days later I received a report on Bobby which delighted me. My psychiatrist friend Nadine, with whom I had discussed him from time to time since the beginning of his treatment, wrote a report on him at this stage. She started by giving an outline of Bobby's problems when he was first referred to us, and then went on:

> Bobby at five, after eight and a half months of treatment, is an attractive child of normal physical development for his age and no motor impairment except for a hesitant speech

pattern and confusion of personal pronouns. He can now communicate verbally with intelligence. He can relate appropriately with affection and body contact, or with appropriate anger by screeching, spitting and shouting. Physical fighting is confined to his brother and mother. His public behaviour, though still unusual, is more acceptable. He has total eye contact, laughs, has a good sense of humour and a sense of concern for people. He shows and verbalizes spontaneous affection for both his parents. He is only just beginning to develop relationships with peers because of limited opportunity.

Bobby's intelligence is high, with a focus on mechanical things. His knowledge of subway maps is considerable and he has a fascination for the New York subway system. He had good musical ability with absolute pitch. Nappies were removed early in treatment and only three incidents of incontinence have occurred.

When I recently re-read this report I was again delighted, not just because of the growth it described in Bobby; I knew he had grown. What it did was to answer in simple but professionally acceptable terms most of the questions that I have been asked by interested professionals over the last four years. I realize that the correct way of keeping records would have been to fill in a questionnaire every week, with sub-headings like 'Eye contact', 'Verbal ability', etc. I have never succeeded in doing this. To me the form-filling process is not related to doctoring, therapy, or listening in any way that I can see. I have watched doctors giving and have my-self given medical examinations for legal or pension purposes; the patient as a person is mostly absent from this process.

When I am involved with therapy or, as I prefer to call it, releasing obstacles to natural growth, my attention is placed somewhere totally other than on any of the items that might be on a form. To me the patient is a prisoner in a cage, a strong person whose strength is being obstructed. My job is to help to remove the obstruction and I want no form-filling to mar this process.

Over the last few months the changes in Bobby had been dramatic. I was going to have to leave, and was wondering when the right moment to leave would be. This is always a problem for a therapist; how do you know when the party is over? In the case of Bobby, as I have already said, I would have liked it to go on much longer.

Bobby helped to provide the answer. He had returned to the womb more than once with Mimi and me, both in the lake and when he lay on the floater with such beautiful abandon in the Los Angeles swimming pool. Now he began to follow up these womb-like scenes with the drama of birth. One day, sitting on my lap, Bobby began to slide down head first, landing upon the floor between my legs. At first, I couldn't think what he was doing; then suddenly I realized that he was acting out being born.

I must have referred to this in some way in my conversations with Robert. He replied that, triggered off by Abigail's birth, both boys had for some time played at being born with their mother. This came as a great surprise to me; I had not thought of them doing anything so intimate with her.

During this winding-up period both Bobby and Billy regularly played 'being born' from Mimi and me, and this seemed to strike a symbolic note. The boys were re-born, and they could start a new life without me.

In late November, Bobby spent the morning waiting for me, and when we met he gave me a tangerine. Later, Robert told me Bobby had asked him for the tangerine 'to give to Rachel'. To my knowledge, it was the first 'present' Bobby ever gave anyone.

End of Sheba (by Mimi)
Bobby's friendship with my boyfriend's dog Sheba had continued for many weeks and we had had many happy outings with her. Suddenly they were brought to a halt. It was my

fault. One day I was out absent-mindedly walking Sheba, who was not on a leash. We were on the sidewalk next to the Park when she crossed a road ahead of me just before the light changed. As the traffic started to pour between us I stood there, stupid with fear, unable to remedy the situation, and terrified that she would try to cross the road back again to join me, which she did.

A sedan driven by a lone man crunched into her a second after she stepped into the road. The man drove on, and Sheba ran into the Park, but she was hurt too badly to live for long. Another dog-walker stayed with her while I ran home to get my boyfriend. When we returned, Sheba died in her master's arms.

The next time I saw Bobby I told him the news of Sheba's death, with full particulars of how it happened. He showed no sense of personal loss, but very gravely told me: 'Mimi, get another dog. You'll have to take care of this one!' He wanted to talk to her master as well, so we phoned him at work. Bobby said briefly, 'I'm very sorry your dog is dead,' waited to hear the reply, then handed the phone to me without further comment.

A few days later I was in a cab with Bobby, Billy and their father, *en route* to Robert's office Christmas party, and I saw we were going to travel over the spot where Sheba got killed, and pointed it out to them.

'Watch out, Sheba!' said Bobby, and I took a cue from him to dramatize the situation.

'Watch out! Oh, no! *Pow!*' I shouted, and tears came to my eyes, remembering.

The boys wanted to have it played over again and again, so I did. Over and over, Sheba and the car met with a 'Pow!' By grown-up standards this may have looked like a macabre entertainment to the boys, but the performance helped me to get my guilt feelings out in the open. Once again, Bobby had called forth a replay of a painful situation until it no longer had the power to hurt.

I felt Robert staring at the three of us as if this was all in terribly bad taste, and what kind of masochist was I anyway, but he didn't interfere. He probably did see the value of what was going on, though he himself tended to be less demonstrative. We played Sheba getting killed a few more times after that day, but never with the same drama as in the taxi.

The very day after the accident, Bobby and I had a loss of another kind, when Rachel left. She had been talking about going for some time, but it hadn't sunk in that this was reality. Over the last nine months the Rachel-Mimi-Bobby-Billy pattern had become so woven into my life that I couldn't really envisage it changing. Then, suddenly, Rachel was there one day and gone the next.

End of Rachel (by Rachel)
My decision to leave New York on 19 December was a sudden one, like diving into a swimming pool after lingering tentatively on the edge for almost too long.

I stayed the last night with Bobby's family, and they gave me a warm send-off. I had explained to Bobby and Billy that I was going, and they took the news quite happily, asking me questions about England.

As I walked out sadly afterwards, through the foyer, I said to the regular security guard there, 'Well, this is me finished. I'm on my way back to England.'

To my surprise, he clasped me warmly by the hand and said, 'I want to thank you from the bottom of my heart for what you have done for that boy.'

In the plane on the way home it struck me as the final irony that this had been said to me by, of all people, a security guard!

Postscript

Bobby paid two visits to England after my return from the U.S. The first was in 1978, when he was six years old. I waited, filled with apprehension, for his train to arrive at Victoria Station. Perhaps he would greet me with hostility; a situation I well knew how to handle by receiving the hostility as love, but would have preferred to handle without his father being present.

'Hi, Bobby,' I said as I spied him.

'I'm not Bobby, I'm Robert.' But he was very happy to see me. He was still the same old Bobby, disappearing and reappearing as soon as we entered the hotel. I took him to my flat, and observed his behaviour: a fierce need to explore the nature of things; a firm repudiation of everything he did not find interesting. His stance and movements had become at first sight completely normal. In his speech he still had some difficulty with pronouns, but otherwise he talked so normally that at least one person we met found his conversation no different from that of any other child of six.

He stayed for a month. By the time he left he knew by heart the entire London Underground and all the bus routes; sometimes sitting up until three o'clock in the morning, surrounded by pieces of paper, mapping these details and noting the connections.

His second visit was in the spring of 1979. We met at Wembley Stadium, when he came running up and gave me a big hug.

On both these occasions he met various friends of mine, and made a strong impression on all of them. Joan, a professional pianist, remarked afterwards that Bobby had 'the most vibrant of faces. It was unusual; not the vibrancy of happiness usually associated with children's faces, but the vibrancy of questioning and continual awareness.'

Another friend of mine, Rita, acted as hostess to Bobby and myself. Afterwards she wrote: 'Rachel came to stay, bringing Bobby, an appealing, bright, attractive child of six years. I realized that there was something a bit "different" about him . . . I liked the way he didn't accept and respect matters without question, but did accept and respect our real and, I hope, reasonable explanations. He rejected the food which we prepared, preferring to rummage around in the fridge. He brought a large piece of cheese to one meal, intent on cutting chunks off it. Michael, my husband, said it was all right to have the cheese but would he wash his hands first. There was no argument. He loved to fiddle with the knobs on the television set, rapidly changing channels. We explained that this was probably damaging to the set. It was clear that he desperately wished to continue this activity, but he did stop, with no fuss. I got the impression that his bed-time was very flexible. Our children at that time had a fairly rigid bed-time, perhaps 8.30 or 9 p.m. Rachel said to Bobby "In this house, this is the time you go to bed." Again there was no argument.

'There were two incidents which were less than pleasant. I was once in the kitchen chatting to my daughter when Bobby burst in and sank his teeth into her arm. I don't know what led to this outburst, but I remember feeling that it was unacceptable behaviour. Another day I asked Bobby if he wanted some lunch. He said no. I made something on toast for everyone else. When he saw the meal he flew into a rage and started banging a plate on the table. I hadn't realized that he wanted just toast. I found this over-reaction a bit bizarre. In the few days Bobby was with us I didn't feel he made a relationship with any of us, but I noticed that besides being aggressive at times towards Rachel he was also very loving and affectionate towards her. I also noticed his care over certain matters. He found a bike lying near our house. After use he carefully parked it in the place where bikes stayed . . . there were several incidents like this.'

Bobby also met a young criminal lawyer called Lucy. When I began to tell her the methods my team of helpers used with Bobby, she stopped me. 'I'll build my own personal relationship with him. I want us to be totally independent of your team,' she said. She wrote: 'Bobby and I used to go out together every Sunday, and sometimes also during the week . . . There were two things that he really liked to do when he was with me: travelling on the Underground and going to the adventure playground at Parliament Hill Fields. Generally we used to go to the adventure playground, because I had very mixed feelings about travelling with Bobby on the Underground. I, like many British people, consider that the proper way to behave on public transport is to keep quiet and not to disturb other people, in the hope that other people will keep quiet and not disturb me. I have a particular dislike for people with young children who allow the children to run riot and make no effort to subdue them. Because of this, whenever I travelled with Bobby on the tube I used to be well aware of the venomous glances that were being directed at me, which I considered to be perfectly justified. Nonetheless I also immensely enjoyed his enthusiasm and the pleasure that he got from his travels on the train. He would stand by the sliding doors; he would announce to the people inside the train what station we had reached and what lines intersected at that station. He would then, when the doors had opened, announce to the people standing outside where the train was going and what lines it would intersect with further along the route. All this would be said very fast in his strong American accent. Bobby was not playing at being a guide, he was *being* a guide. He was not looking for admiration or approval or amusement; he quite clearly thought of himself as providing a service. He didn't get into conversation with other people, generally because anybody who did address him did so in a patronizing way that quite clearly he found infuriating.

'One of the reasons that I didn't like the train trip was that from time to time Bobby would try to hold the train doors open, when the guard had pushed the button to close them. He would also try and prise them open between stations. Once I had explained to him how much this particular behaviour frightened me, he didn't do it so often, but I could see that the hankering was there.

'It was while I travelled around with Bobby that I realized how strongly bound by convention I was. Habits of politeness and superficial consideration for others in public came naturally to me, and I suppose by and large I approve of these habits. Bobby, however, has no such restraints. It would not be right to say that he was cheeky or deliberately offensive, although from time to time he certainly did offend people. Cheekiness to me implies a wish to annoy, and a realization that the person to whom one is cheeky expects to be treated with respect. Most adults expect to be treated with respect by most children. Bobby, I think, had no particular respect for adults in general, although it would not be true to say that he had disrespect for them either.

'I particularly remember one occasion when he and I were sitting on a bus. The driver had got off and closed the automatic doors behind him, and we were left to wait for the new driver to come and open the doors again. Bobby started getting restless at this and tried to prise open the doors. I had every sympathy with him. He also started complaining about what had happened, which I also sympathized with. One of the other passengers then said to him, 'What a noisy little boy you are,' in a tone obviously intended to rebuke both of us. Immediately Bobby turned around and said 'Shut up, you fucker.' The silence that followed was profound. I think I found myself more tempted then than at any other time to explain that Bobby was not like other children, and that he was not deliberately offensive. However, I realized that if I had made that explanation I would have been betraying him, and I would only have been doing so to save my own embarrassment. I managed to hang on with him until the relief driver arrived, and then got off the bus with Bobby, feeling both embarrassed and elated at what had happened.

'He liked going to the adventure playground because there was a big wooden model steam engine which he could play in, and because the playground was alongside a railway line, and trains went past about every twenty minutes or so. Bobby knew all the head codes of the trains and could tell me where they started and finished, and which stations they stopped at. He would 'drive' the wooden train all over the Underground system, often by himself but occasionally with one or two other children whom he roped into his obsession. He would always talk very fast, stuttering and jumping up and down in an effort to get the words out faster. He was quite single-minded, and could not be distracted, although his mind could be changed.

'I wanted to get my own way sometimes, as well, and had to negotiate a way with Bobby to this end. A particular problem was dirty hands and face. I didn't really mind how dirty his hands got, but sometimes I could hardly bear to look at the mess on his face. He had a real aversion to washing. To begin with I used to ask him to wash his face by saying 'It's not very nice to have a dirty face, is it?' or 'Wouldn't you like to have a nice clean face?' This cut no ice with Bobby, because obviously he found it very nice to have a dirty face, and not at all nice to have a clean face. It was only when I explained to him that I didn't like it, that we could open negotiations as to how often it was going to be cleaned, or how much of it was going to be cleaned. It was not, I think, that Bobby was concerned that my likes and dislikes should be pandered to. It was simply that he was so conscious of his own very powerful likes and dislikes that he accepted mine as being equally powerful, and acknowledged that sometimes they must prevail. I think we hit a fairly good balance. Generally we did what he wanted, because he wanted things so desperately, but we hardly ever did anything that I really didn't want. He always knew that he was free to go off and do things on his own, but generally he preferred to stay with me, and so we would find something that we would both like to do. There was no coercion in our relationship. I wasn't in a position to make him do anything he didn't want to do, or to make him feel guilty or ashamed of his behaviour, or frightened of my response to him . . . he was open to me as long as I accepted our basic equality.

'We seldom talked about personal things, but I do remember once walking along Camden High Street with him, hand in hand, and him saying to me, 'Lucy, am I your friend?' I was very moved by this, because at that time I was in a relationship with somebody where I felt very insecure, and I was conscious of the anxious caution revealed in Bobby's words. It seemed clear to me that behind all the explosive talk and action there was another sort of activity, which I felt was probably much too delicate for me to attempt to involve myself with.

'Bobby and I used to have a really good time. He would make immense demands upon me, and hardly ever say thank you, but I knew that he enjoyed being with me very much indeed, and would like to be with me more often. Because of what I saw in his behaviour with other people, I felt that if I had been sloppy or lazy in my response to him he would have rejected me very quickly, and I was grateful to him for showing me how difficult it is, and how rewarding, truly to attend to somebody.'

At the time of Bobby's second visit to England my friend Hazel, who is involved in experimental theatre, and had seen my work with children, readily agreed to join the team of helpers who would be with Bobby on his visit. She writes: 'As this was Bobby's second time in England, his knowledge of

London's transport systems was already extensive. In our first few days together, I tried to direct our route, but stopped when I realized that Bobby had ideas of his own. It was his prerogative; all Hours belonged to him.

'Bobby was like no-one else I had ever met. He was very direct, which was often disarming, and constantly on the move. In the Underground carriages he would run up and down, pressing all the buttons and switches he could find. He was completely fearless.

'His seriousness impressed me. For instance, each evening when he got home to have supper he would open his map and trace where he had been that day, or might be going tomorrow. He would draft everything meticulously on paper, marking out the Underground route and how it connected with the bus route, showing this by joining squares representing the tube stations, with the corresponding bus numbers below. All his spelling was correct. During the course of his drawing, which he referred to as his work, he would pause for interludes when he would walk and hop in a straight line, turning and repeating this many times, his arms held stiffly at his sides and his fingers stretched grotesquely, poking at the air or dangling from a limp wrist. I was aware that his seriousness was an obstacle to his making friends with other children. There were times when he tried to approach them, but it was not with ease. It was all the more difficult when they mimicked his Americanisms. On a few occasions I noticed that he was not comfortable in apparently happy public gatherings. He told me that he did not like people laughing because he imagined that they were laughing at him. Yet he could easily make contact with people on the street, and converse freely with anyone. Therefore, after a month of being in London, he was allowed to spend entire days on his own, coming in sometimes as late as midnight. He was then seven years old. No one felt alarm waiting for his return; they just accepted it. He was a responsible, fearless young person, with all his wits about him, knowing very well the art of survival.

'When I arrived in the morning I would not know whether I would be with Bobby for the day or if he would want to go off on his own. His need to be alone became progressively more frequent, and when this happened, breakfast-time with him became especially important for me. During this period Bobby's only interest appeared to be London's transport systems, and I began to wonder what else he could become interested in if I took the initiative. Most children of his age respond to stories, so one morning I asked him if he knew the story of "Jack and the Beanstalk". He said he did not. Although realizing that this initiative was contrary to Rachel's normal approach, I told him the story. At the end he was full of questions: "Why was the family so poor?" "Why was Jack's mother so angry?" "What was his father like?" and so on. Finally he said abruptly that he must be going, because it was getting late.

'Next morning he greeted me as if he were the mother in the story, saying sharply: "Why did you sell the cow for beans, you stupid boy?" I immediately took on the role of Jack, and was sent to bed without any supper. The following day, he became Jack and I was the mother; there was much romping and laughter. Next day I extended the game, suggesting that we should write the story line by line in turns until it was complete. This he happily agreed to. In fact I only provided the connecting words; he wrote the story. Rachel overheard us, and when Bobby had left she told me that it had been his first full directed session.

'In the summer, Rachel asked me to take Bobby back to his parents in New York. When we arrived he was thrilled to be re-united with his family. His camaraderie with his brother was exceptional; they moved together with the speed of light. He was also extremely affectionate towards his little sister, constantly picking her up and hugging her.

'In New York Bobby was not allowed to enjoy the freedom he had known in London. He was always accompanied by an adult. His parents, moreover, had neither the time nor the energy to give him the facilities to which he had grown accustomed, so there were tantrums which sometimes took hours to overcome. At other times, however, as when the family talked about their intended move to California, excellent conversations developed with the boys. This was my first visit to New York, and I realized that Bobby was a true native of the city. It projects an image of dynamic, virile energy, and Bobby himself seemed to epitomize this.'

Meg, a remedial teacher, spent about two weeks with Hazel and Bobby in New York that summer. She had first met him briefly in England earlier in the year. 'I was eager', she writes, 'to take the opportunity of seeing more of Bobby, especially on his home ground. During those two weeks Hazel and I were on holiday with Bobby rather than giving him Special Times. Each morning the three of us would discuss what we were going to do for the day. Tantrums sometimes resulted, but not always serious ones, and we invariably reached an agreement, often a compromise, on the day's programme. I was aware how much Bobby had progressed in gradually coming to respect the ideas and wishes of others, and not just doing what he wanted all the time. One day he insisted that we should go to the central bus terminal in New York, arguing that this would be a really worthwhile experience to British tourists. We protested that there were far more interesting sights for us to see, particularly considering the short length of our stay. After a long discussion we ended up going to the Statue of Liberty!

'On two occasions Hazel and I dared to presume that we knew best which bus or train we had to catch. Both times, Bobby became quite desperate, screaming that we were wrong, and both times Bobby was right. Thinking back, I can understand his frustration. We did a lot of walking in New York that summer, and when Bobby was involved in something else Hazel and I would talk. He was often in a world of his own, but at times was aware of our conversations. Frequently he would walk quite close to us, with a pizza, or a hot dog, and a can of pop. Or he would race ahead and we would find him going round and round in a revolving door. Sometimes he trailed behind, running his finger along the railings, and occasionally catching up to say: "Don't talk psychology!" but he was never agitated or annoyed.

'I had a marvellous time in New York with Bobby and Hazel, and felt the richness of the experience, as one does when something is shared with good friends. For me, Bobby had become a good friend, and the closeness I felt with him was probably expressed most fully by the cuddles that he initiated, and that I enjoyed. It seemed to me that there had been genuine communication on many different levels, and I particularly appreciated his sense of humour. This had been my first visit to the U.S. and, looking back, I feel I have been privileged in that my memories of it were vividly coloured by Bobby's presence.'

Bobby's rapid movement was something which impressed everybody. Kate, a clinical psychologist, whom we visited unexpectedly, wrote: 'I opened the door to Rachel and a child, and he positively shot up to my fourth floor; he wanted so much to be *in*. I have never seen anything like it.'

A small incident which occurred one day when I walked with Bobby to a friend's house, which stands on a corner, struck me as significant. As we drew near to her home, Bobby asked me, 'Is Fanny's house on the next corner?' I replied: 'I think so, I'm not sure,' whereupon he flew into a tantrum. Bobby has no concept of half-knowledge – a concept which most adults live with all the time. He needs to feel he has absolute knowledge, in the same way that some musicians have absolute pitch.

In a letter which I received from Bobby's father, dated 29 October 1982, he wrote: 'Bobby continues to do well at his special school, and gets progressively better at fitting in socially. The current prognosis by the school is that at the end of the school year (or perhaps the next) he may be able to make the transition to a regular school. He has been taking piano lessons for the last six months, and though he characteristically shows little enthusiasm on the surface, he has impressive musical aptitude, and is progressing very well. Both he and Billy got adult-sized ten-speed bicycles for their birthdays a few weeks ago.'

Most recently, Lucy called on Bobby in California in the winter of 1982. Bobby was by then aged ten.

Her first reaction was one of shock. He appeared to have conformed, matured and filled out physically; it seemed that the old Bobby had disappeared. Her sense of loss conveyed itself to me over the trans-Atlantic telephone, and I mourned with her. But when she took him out, away from his family and his school, she suddenly found herself totally at ease with him, making contact with the old, inner Bobby: indestructible and intact. What she had seen at first were fragments of social behaviour learned at his special education school.

There is no need to mourn Bobby. The real, magical soul, set free by Bobby's hard work and that of Mimi and the rest of our team, is still there and will always be there.

Select Bibliography

The most important influence on the work described in this book was Dr. Margaret Lowenfeld, and of course I would like to give details of her books but, alas, she died with her major work unpublished. Readers who are interested in her work should consult the collection of her papers in the archives of the University of Cambridge, where many of her unpublished manuscripts are in process of being deposited. Her only published book on this subject is: *Play in Childhood* (Victor Gollancz, 1935), now out of print.

Other relevant publications

Dibs: in Search of Self. Virginia Axline (Victor Gollancz, 1966, Pelican Books, 1971)

Magical Child, Joseph Chilton Pearce (Granada Publishing Ltd., 1977)

The Continuum Concept, Jean Liedloff (Gerald Duckworth, 1975, Futura Publications, 1976)

Son Rise, Barry Neil Kaufman (Warner Books, New York, 1977)

Children with Emerald Eyes, Mira Rothenberg (Dial Press, New York, 1960, Souvenir Press, London, 1978)

The Children of the Dream, Bruno Bettelheim (Thames & Hudson, 1969, Granada, 1971)

The Empty Fortress, Bruno Bettelheim (Free Press, New York, Collier-McMillan, West Drayton, 1967)

'Autistic' Children – new hope for a cure, N. & E. A. Tinbergen (Allen & Unwin, 1983)

'Autism', article in *ENC. Alternative Medicine and Self-help*, Anastasia Prescott (Hutchinson, 1978)

The One-to-One Relationship in the Treatment of Autistic Children M. H. Dundas, *Acta Paedopsychiatra*, 1968. vol. 35, fas. 4–8, pp. 242–5

The Siege, Clara Clairborne Park (Colin Smyth, 1968)